HOSTAGE

Notorious Irish Kidnappings

Paul Howard

THE O'BRIEN PRESS

DUBLIN

First published 2004 by The O'Brien Press Ltd,
20 Victoria Road, Dublin 6, Ireland.
Tel: +353 1 4923333; Fax: +353 1 4922777
E-mail: books@obrien.ie
Website: www.obrien.ie

ISBN: 0-86278-769-6

British Library Cataloguing-in-Publication Data
Howard, Paul
Hostage : notorious Irish kidnappings
1.Kidnapping - Ireland - History - 20th century
I.Title
364.1'54'09415

1 2 3 4 5 6 7 8 9 10
04 05 06 07 08

Layout and design: The O'Brien Press Ltd.
Printing: Nørhaven Paperback A/S

Picture Credits
Front cover, clockwise from left: Shergar, Ben Dunne, © copyright Derek Speirs,
Report; Tiede Herrema, courtesy of the Sunday Tribune. Back cover (top), Don Tidey,
© copyright Eamon Farrell, Photocall Ireland. Picture section: p1, © copyright Derek
Speirs, Report; p2 (top and bottom), Independent Newspapers; p3 (top), Press
Association, (bottom), Independent Newspapers; p4 (top and bottom), Independent
Newspapers; p5 (top and bottom), Colman Doyle; p6 (top and bottom), Independent
Newspapers; p7 (top), courtesy of Fr Dermod McCarthy, (bottom), Independent
Newspapers; p8, Independent Newspapers.

Acknowledgements

Given the sensitive nature of much of the material in this book, a number of people agreed to be interviewed only on the grounds of anonymity. Sincerest thanks are due to my IRA and Garda sources who were very generous with their time and recollections. Several people declined interview requests. But I would like to thank Eddie Gallagher, Phil Flynn, Nicky Kehoe, James Murphy, Ben Dunne and Don Tidey for very politely explaining their reasons for not wishing to speak and for suffering, with good humour, my repeated efforts to change their minds.

For the time they took to share their, in some cases, painful memories with me, I would like to thank the following: Captain Sean Berry, Stan Cosgrove, Paddy Cooney, Roy David, Alan Dukes, Garret FitzGerald, Mark Hely-Hutchinson, Jonathan Irwin, Father Dermod McCarthy, Judy Maxwell, Freddie Murphy, Harold O'Sullivan, Derek Thompson and most especially Dr Tiede Herrema. Thank you also to all the staff at The O'Brien Press, especially Mary Webb, a great editor whose enthusiasm for this book helped fire mine.

Dedication

For Ken Finlay

Contents

1. They Shoot Horses, Don't They?
The Disappearance of Shergar   **page 11**

2. Kidnapping by the Book
Lord and Lady Donoughmore   **75**

3. Eddie Gallagher's Last Stand
The Taking of Tiede Herrema   **120**

4. Prisoner in Bandit Country
The Kidnapping of Ben Dunne   **185**

5. Shoot-Out at Derrada Wood
Don Tidey's Ordeal   **215**

Bibliography   **252**

INTRODUCTION

Kidnapping was the crime of the 1970s. Dozens of high pro-file cases made the news in Europe, the United States and South America. John Paul Getty III, the teenage grandson of the American oil tycoon, was snatched by an Italian gang, who cut off his ear to advance their demand for a ransom. Patty Hearst, daughter of the millionaire publisher Ran-dolph Hearst, was kidnapped by the hard-line revolution-ary Symbionese Liberation Army, who demanded that foodstuffs be distributed to the poor of San Francisco. In London, Princess Anne narrowly escaped death when she was shot at by a would-be kidnapper who planned to hold her for a one million pound ransom.

By the early 1980s, kidnapping had become the crime of choice for paramilitary and criminal gangs, who saw it as a way of making easy money, literally overnight. During 1983, in the Republic of Ireland alone, there were eight reported incidents, making it, *per capita*, the most serious rival to Italy, the world kidnapping capital, which had more than 150 cases a year. But, as one Garda source pointed out, the eight they investigated that year were merely the reported ones.

Most of the abductions took place in south Dublin or north Wicklow and the *modus operandi* was almost always the same. In March 1983, the wife of publisher Albert Folens was held hostage at their home in Enniskerry, while her husband was forced to come up with £10,000 for her release. In April, the wife and daughter of steel importer Peter Simms were held at gunpoint in their home in Shankill, until Simms handed over £10,000 in cash when the banks opened the following morning. In June, the wife of Arthur Jones, the managing director of Allied Couriers, was taken from her home in Stillorgan, but was rescued from a house in St Margaret's in north Dublin before a ransom was demanded. In August, solicitor William Somerville was kidnapped from his home in Enniskerry and eventually found tied to a tree on the army firing range in Kilpedder, County Wicklow. In accordance with the kidnappers' demands, a ransom of £50,000 was placed in a burnt-out car in Fassaroe sandpit, but most of the money was subsequently recovered. In October, the wife of Robert Manina, a Canadian industrialist and art collector, was taken hostage at her home in Greystones, and £60,000 demanded from her husband.

Some of these jobs were the work of Michael Boyle, an armed robber and drug dealer from Bray, County Wicklow, and of other criminal gangs.

When the Provisionals came into the game the stakes became considerably higher ...

CHAPTER ONE

They Shoot Horses, Don't They?
The Disappearance of Shergar

'Those hoors are up to no good.' Steve Dunne

It was just before four o'clock in the morning on 7 February, 1983 when Freddie Murphy pulled his taxi onto the rank at Aston Quay in Dublin city centre. Business was sluggish even for a Monday night and he resigned himself to having to sit out the two or three hours before the airport snapped into life again. He bought two newspapers, the *Irish Press* and the *Irish Independent*, their covers dominated by coverage of a challenge to Charles Haughey's leadership of Fianna Fáil by his old foe, Des O'Malley. But he only had time to scan the headlines before there was a tap on his window. Two men stood there. One, in his mid twenties, got into the back of the car. The other, who was older, forty or over, with a pocked complexion and wearing a black coat and gloves, sat in the front passenger seat next to Murphy. Both were from Dublin. Twenty years driving a taxi had sharpened Murphy's instinct for trouble. 'There was something bogey about them,' he remembers. 'The second they got into the car, I regretted ever opening the door to them.'

They asked to be taken to Finglas, a twenty-minute drive north of the city, but they didn't have an address. 'Just head out that direction,' the older man said. Murphy tried to engage them in conversation. He figured they might be dockworkers, and asked them whether they'd just finished work for the night. The older man answered in an offhand way that told Murphy he had no interest in talking. When they reached Finglas, they gave him directions into Gortdeg Park, a housing estate that faces the council refuse dump. 'We were running out of houses,' Murphy remembers, 'and I was thinking, "I know what's going down here".'

He was told to pull in. A car passed in the opposite direction and the two men rummaged through their pockets and made a big play of arguing over who was going to pay the £2.65 fare. Murphy had been mugged enough times to know what was coming next. He opened the door and tried to get out. But in his panic his feet became entangled in the pedals, and the older man took him by the scruff of the neck and pulled him back into the car. He felt something hard pressed against the back of his head, which he took to be a gun. 'Take it easy,' the man beside him said. 'All we're after is the car. You'll get it back.' The young man took the gun away and told Murphy to get out. He didn't stand around long enough to see his pale green Ford Granada being driven away at high speed.

The previous day, Pat Kelly, a farmer from Kilcurry, less than a mile from the border in County Louth, looked out of his window at 10.30am and noticed that his double-axle horsebox was gone. It had been stolen during the night.

❖❖❖

Poor John Matthias thought he'd won the Derby. When he tore around Tattenham Corner, he knew *Glint of Gold* had enough left in his legs to hold off any of the horses behind him. He got into the home straight, charged past the finishing post and punched the air in delight. It was only as he was reining in his horse that he realised that another horse had crossed the line ahead of him. The margin of Shergar's victory was stunning. One minute it was a race, the next a procession. Walter Swinburn, the young jockey who, like his mount, forged his reputation that day, was looking over his shoulder in amazement all the way to the line. Officially, the margin was ten lengths – the biggest winning margin in the history of the race – but Swinburn had been pulling Shergar up long before the finish. It was difficult to find fault with the view of John McCrirrick, that excitable eccentric of race broadcasting, who declared, 'This is the horse of the century.'

Shergar was born three years earlier, in 1978, at the Sheshoon Stud in County Kildare, owned by his highness Prince Karim El Husseini Shah, the Aga Khan, who was the leader of the world's twenty million Ismaili Muslims. The horse came from impeccable stock, part of a pedigree line established by the Aga Khan's grandfather in the 1920s, when the family started its international breeding empire. Shergar's father was *Great Nephew*, a famous big race winner in France before he went to stud.

But the horse generated little enthusiasm as a foal. Sent to the Beach Hurst Stable in Newmarket to be trained by Michael Stoute, he looked no better than average. He won his first race as a two-year-old, but then a two-and-a-half length defeat in the William Hill Futurity, the only other race he ran in 1980, had him written off as a classic prospect.

The spring of 1981 saw the horse reborn. The first indication that it was going to be a special year came in April, when he won the Sundown Classic Trial by ten clear lengths. In his last race before the Derby, he romped home in the Chester Vase twelve lengths clear and was installed as the white-hot favourite for Epsom. But no one could have predicted how effortless his victory would look. Micheál O'Hehir, the respected Irish racing commentator, compared him to *Nijinsky*, popularly believed to be the greatest racehorse ever. Within days, pieces of the foaling box in which Shergar was reared were being sold to collectors.

Aesthetically, he was a far from perfect specimen, with a depth of girth that made his forelegs look short, and a gallop that had a slight scratching action to it. But veteran horsewatchers were impressed by the way the horse held himself, his proud bearing suggesting he knew just how great he was. He had what the racing journalist Colin Turner described as 'a Roman head that he carried in such a cocky way that you had to smile.'

After the Derby he stormed to victory in the Irish Sweepstakes Derby, then in the King George VI and Queen Elizabeth Stakes at Ascot under Lester Piggott, winning by four lengths. The Queen Elizabeth Diamond Stakes in July at Ascot was Shergar's first battle with older horses and a test of his claim to all-time greatness. It wasn't Swinburn's cleverest race. He spent too long hugging the inside and, after the home turn, with barely two furlongs left, he was shut in.

Lester Piggot looked best placed to win on *Light Cavalry*, but suddenly a gap opened up as Piggot rolled off the rails, Swinburn aimed the horse through it, past Light Cavalry and Master Willie, and accelerated clear for his fifth successive win of the season.

The Prix de l'Arc de Triomphe, Europe's richest race, was targeted for the autumn, but Shergar didn't make it that far. He was roundly beaten in the St Leger at Doncaster, failing to finish in the first three. The Aga Khan decided it was time to retire him and cash in on his reputation by putting him out to stud. The expectation was that he'd be sent to America to sire great racehorses there. It was a genuine shock when the Aga Khan announced that he'd stand at Ballymany Stud in County Kildare, just three miles away from the pastures where he was reared. It was a huge boost to the bloodstock industry in Ireland.

Stoute was heartbroken to see Shergar go, and not because he delivered him his first Derby success as a trainer. He and his family had developed a love for the animal, with its gentle nature and warmth towards humans, especially children. 'He was a good natured animal,' according to Stan Cosgrove, his vet when he returned to Ireland. 'Easy to handle, with a very trusting nature.'

Stoute drove the horse to Cambridge airport himself and helped load him onto a plane for the journey home. Bunting hung across the streets in Newbridge to welcome him. The local cubs and brownies, scouts and guides, marched behind a brass band in a procession watched by thousands of flag-waving locals, who lined the streets for a glimpse of the extraordinary animal.

Alan Dukes, the minister for finance, was a keen racegoer and was excited at the thought of one of the world's most famous racehorses coming to Ballymany at the heart of his constituency. Dukes brought a group of Dáil colleagues to the stud to see the animal, which had had a £10m valuation placed on it. Dukes has fond memories of the occasion:

> We were all standing around looking at him, this incredible horse, and I remember the late Paudge Brennan saying to me, 'Think about it, lads. Each one of them legs is worth two-and-a-half-million pounds.' And I said to him, 'No, Paudge, it's the one you can't see that's worth all the money'.

Owning a share in a horse with Shergar's reputation was like having a licence to print money. A simple nomination to the stallion cost £35,000, with a further £35,000 payable if he managed to put the mare into foal. And the horse proved to be extraordinarily fecund. Forty of the forty-two mares he covered in 1982 had foals.

The Aga Khan sold thirty-three shares in the horse at a quarter of a million pounds each and kept a further seven back for himself. The membership of the syndicate was a *Who's Who* of the international business and bloodstock worlds. It included Stavros Niarchos, the Greek shipping billionaire and brother-in-law of Aristotle Onassis; Sir Philip Oppenheimer, the diamond magnate and jeweller to the British royal family; Sir Robert McAlpine, the famous construction tycoon, and Robert Sangster, the pools million-aire. The leading trainer, Vincent O'Brien, and his son-in-law, John Magnier, also bought shares.

In February 1983, Ghislain Drion, the French-born

manager of Ballymany, was finalising arrangements to receive the fifty-five mares due to be covered between the middle of the month and the middle of July. They included some of the most valuable horses in Europe, such as 1,000 Guineas winner *On The House* and the Prix de l'Arc winner, *Akiyda*. The syndicate stood to make between £3.5m and £4m from Shergar that year. On the day that Freddie Murphy's taxi was stolen, the first day of the breeding season was only a week away.

❖❖❖

Tuesday, 8 February 1983 began like any other day for Jimmy Fitzgerald, the head groom at Ballymany. He got up at 6.30am to feed Shergar and the other horse in the stallion box, which was a five-minute walk away from his front door. The horses had oats for their morning feed, followed by gowla, a mixture of dried grass and bran. As a treat, he occasionally gave Shergar some apple cider, which the horse loved. At 7.30am, he sat down with his wife, Madge, and their six children for his own breakfast. Fitzgerald was devoted to his work. He'd spent all of his fifty-three years living on the 220-acre stud right on the edge of the Curragh, and was proud to be continuing a tradition that his father started when he worked as head groom to the old Aga Khan back in the 1920s. After breakfast, he checked the staff as they arrived for work. The rest of the day went much the same as any other.

At 6pm the Fitzgerald family sat down to dinner. While they ate, the pale green Ford Granada stolen from Murphy, and now bearing number plates from a motorcycle stolen in

Dun Laoghaire, was on its way to Ballymany, along with a cream-coloured Ford Transit van and a brown Hillman Hunter that was towing the stolen horsebox. The convoy of vehicles turned off the main Dublin to Cork road and continued on towards the Curragh. Fitzgerald finished his dinner, then visited the stallion house where he made his last check on the horses for the night.

Peter Cullen, the deputy groom at Ballymany, lived with his wife, Liz, in a cottage a hundred yards away from the Fitzgerald home. That night, the couple had arranged to go for a drink in O'Rourke's in Newbridge with their daughter, Alicia, and her husband, Steve. Alicia noticed a car and a horsebox parked at the side of the road that skirts Ballymany, though in that part of the world it was a far from unusual sight. But when they left for Newbridge twenty minutes later, they witnessed something that did strike them as suspicious. There were three men hanging around outside the main gate to the stud, two on the opposite side of the road and one on the near side. Liz, who got out of the car to shut the gate, thought the scene so odd that she took a long look at the men and made sure to remember them. The one nearest to her was dressed like a Garda, wearing a hat with a peak on it and a dark, tunic-type coat with a white belt. One of the two on the opposite side of the road was small in stature, had dark wavy hair and a moustache and was wearing jeans and a denim jacket that was unbuttoned; he had his hands in his pockets. The third man was in his mid twenties, of average height, with a very large nose, and was wearing a dark brown anorak. Steve looked at them and said, 'Those hoors are up to no good.'

The Fitzgeralds were watching television. The stolen taxi was parked on a quiet road at the back of the stud and one of its two occupants was using a radio to monitor Garda movements in the area. The horsebox was parked at the entrance to the neighbouring Griffin Stud. All the pieces were in place. But, at the last minute, there was almost a hitch in the operation. The two men in the taxi saw what they thought was a Garda walking towards the car. The man was driving past when he noticed two dead sheep on the road and went to ask them if the car had been in an accident. The driver, who was stout and dressed in a combat jacket, said he hadn't noticed any sheep. The occupant of the passenger seat, a small man in a green quilted jacket, appeared nervous. The driver asked the man if he was a Garda, and the man said he wasn't. He was a bus driver who was on his way home from work.

At 8.30pm the operation began. Using a walkie-talkie, one of the three men at the entrance to the stud called up the taxi and the Hillman Hunter with the horsebox. The stud was hidden behind a high boundary wall and a dense thicket of evergreens and birches, but getting into the stable, where one of the world's most valuable horses slept, presented no difficulty. The main gate didn't even have a lock. The man in the peaked hat lifted the latch and let the taxi in, closed the gate behind him and climbed into the car, leaving the Hillman Hunter and the horsebox at the staff entrance a short distance away. The taxi drove up the long snaking driveway towards the groom's house.

Jimmy Fitzgerald was upstairs shaving when he heard the car pull up outside. His twenty-one-year-old son, Bernard, was on the way into the living room when he saw the car's headlights in the driveway. There was a sharp rap on the door and he answered it. The taxi's lights were on full beam, allowing him to see only the silhouettes of the three men. A voice said, 'Is the boss man around?' Bernard turned to call his father but was punched hard in the face and pushed over in the hallway. A man in a balaclava and a hooded green anorak stood over him, holding an Uzi submachine gun to his head. Jimmy heard the ruckus and then the pounding of boots on the stairs. He stepped out onto the landing and was met by a masked man in a brown anorak who was pointing a gun at him. He ordered him downstairs.

Two gunmen had already burst in on Madge and the children in the living room. One of them, wearing a combat jacket and speaking with a Northern Ireland accent, had a pistol. The other, dressed in a grey sweater, carried a walkie-talkie. The family was told to stay calm. Jimmy asked, 'What do you want with us? We haven't done anything to anyone.' He was taken into the kitchen. 'We've come for Shergar,' the man with the walkie-talkie said quietly. He said the horse was being taken for ransom. Fitzgerald remembered him mentioning £1m, though the eventual demand was twice that amount. 'He's worth more,' he was told. 'There'll be no police, or the horse is dead.' In contrast to the composure of his companion, the man with the Northern accent was in a state of high excitement. He paced the kitchen floor, shouting: 'I want Drion's number. I'll ring tomorrow. The codeword is "King Neptune".' Jimmy said he couldn't trust himself to remember it and asked if he could write it down, which he did, on the back cover of a telephone directory.

'Come on, you'll have to get the horse for us,' the man with the walkie-talkie said. Jimmy was marched to the front door of the house and handed over to two of the men the Cullens had seen hanging around earlier – 'The Jockey' and 'The Nose' – as the Gardaí came to call them. They took Jimmy by the arms and marched him through the court-yard in front of his home, past the main stable block, through an archway, past the office where Drion and his staff worked during the day and to the stallion house. A brass plate on the wall outside recorded Shergar's achieve-ments in racing. The car towing the horsebox pulled up. The light in the stable was already on when they arrived, and another man, about six foot in height and wearing a blue boiler suit and a white balaclava, was waiting outside.

Jimmy was asked which of the two horses in the box was Shergar, which was almost certainly a test. It's absurd to think that the gang, having planned the operation with military-style precision, couldn't tell the difference between a bay and a grey. He pointed out Shergar. The man in the white balaclava, who spoke with a Meath accent, said: 'Put whatever he has on him,' and Jimmy attached the horse's collar, bridle and bit, as well as a long lead. The Meath man, who seemed to have a good understanding of horses, asked what Shergar liked to eat. Jimmy told him about the oats and the gowla, and the apple cider he gave him as a treat. He was told to remove his coat and the Meath man put it on over his boiler suit to ensure that, in his unfamiliar new environment, the horse would have the reassuring smell of his groom in his nostrils. The man gathered up armfuls of Shergar's bedding, which he scattered across the floor of the stolen horsebox. It was 8.50pm when Fitzgerald led the horse out into the frosty night air, up the ramp and into the trailer. He took a long look at the horse; he said later that he had a feeling in his gut that it was the last time he would ever see him. Then they were gone. As James Murphy, the Garda superintendent who led the search for the horse, said memorably: 'The horse went quietly.'

'The Nose' and 'The Jockey' took Jimmy back to the house. In the kitchen the man with the Northern accent told him, 'We're taking you with us. We won't harm you if you co-operate.' He had a bad cold and asked for a glass of water, which Jimmy got for him. He was brought back into the living room to tell his family he was being taken as insurance. They were warned not to phone the Gardaí.

An hour after the horse was taken, the remaining members of the gang led Jimmy out of the house and put him in the back of the Transit van. He was ordered to lie on the floor. Two men got in the back with him. The van left Bally-many and turned right, then right again and took the quiet back road towards Kilcock. One of the gang lit a cigarette, and the man with the Northern accent, whom Jimmy took to be the leader, told him to put it out. When they had driven about twenty miles, the van pulled over. Jimmy was instructed to phone Ghislain Drion when he returned home, to tell him the ransom demand would be made the following day. He was told: 'Walk straight on and don't look back. You'll come to a town.'

Jimmy got out. He didn't know where he was, but he ran in the direction they told him and he reached the bridge that crosses the Royal Canal on the way into Kilcock, County

Kildare. It was just before 11pm and the village was deserted. He went to the telephone box outside Ma Byrne's pub, but when he put his hand in his pocket for money he discovered he only had a one-pound note. He got some change at the local Chinese takeaway, then called his brother Des, who arrived quickly. They drove back towards Ballymany, but when they were about a mile short of home, Jimmy, by now deep in shock, asked to be dropped off at a petrol station to walk the rest of the way home and clear his head. A Garda who interviewed him the next day said he had the look of a man who'd stared hell in the face.

❖❖❖

The IRA were in dire need of money at the beginning of 1983. The war in the North had ground to a stalemate and the organisation lacked the hardware to bring about the kind of escalation they wanted. They had no M16 heavy calibre machine guns, for instance, and only a handful of RPG rocket launchers that were supplied by the Libyan leader Colonel Gaddafi in 1972. Noraid (Irish Northern Aid, an American-based organisation formed 'to support Irish political prisoners and their dependents') was still the Provisionals' main source of money, contributing an estimated $1m a year, most of which was spent in the US on weapons that were then shipped to Ireland. But the FBI had recently infiltrated the American arms network that supplied eighty percent of the IRA's arms, while the security forces in the North were seizing an average of more than three hundred guns a year. The Provisionals desperately needed money for arms that would bring the organisation into the 1980s.

According to one British intelligence source from the time:

> Effectively, the IRA were fighting a modern war using Fifties hardware. They had some weapons from Libya, a few rocket launchers and missiles and so forth, but their main weapons were Armalite rifles and homemade explosives, the same as they were using during the old border war. If the war was going to go anywhere, they needed to re-arm. It was as simple as that. If they were going to up the ante, they needed to get their hands on some serious weaponry, and to do that they needed some serious money.

The IRA had a specific arms purchase in mind: the SA-7 Grail Surface to Air Missile system. It was by no means the cutting edge in weaponry. But if they could blow a British army helicopter out of the skies – especially around the northern border areas, where soldiers could no longer use the roads – the IRA could effectively drive the British out of South Armagh. The weapons were Soviet-manufactured and similar to the US-made Redeye. The twenty-pound, heat-seeking missile had a range of five-and-a-half kilometres, a speed of 580 metres per second and had a highly explosive warhead. It was fired from a shoulder-mounted tube, could be reloaded inside seven seconds and had the advantage of being light and portable, the whole apparatus measuring just a metre-and-a-half long and weighing less than ten kilos. The only downside was its price. Each system cost £25,000, but sold for up to four times that amount on the black market. Large numbers of SA-7s had ended up in the hands of terrorist organisations who were better resourced than the IRA. But some of the Aga Khan's millions could finance a sizeable shipment.

Upgrading the IRA's military hardware wasn't the only imperative behind the drive for money. Sinn Féin's successful flirtation with constitutional politics during the 1981 hungers strikes opened up a new front in the IRA's war, defined by Sinn Féin publicity director Danny Morrison as the 'bullet and ballot box' strategy. Many of the Provisionals' most influential thinkers had become politicised while in prison in the 1970s, and the election to Westminster of Bobby Sands, who died after refusing food for sixty-six days, was the catalyst behind a change in course for Sinn Féin. The party contested the 1982 elections for the new Northern Ireland assembly on an abstentionist ticket, and their 64,191 votes ate into the moderate SDLP's support. Gerry Adams's election as MP for West Belfast in the summer of 1983 would strengthen the resolve of the Northern leadership that the war could be won by opening up a new political dimension.

But elections, like surface-to-air missiles, cost money and there were deep misgivings – particularly among the old southern leaders like Ruairí Ó Brádaigh – about funds being diverted away from the military campaign. While the power struggle between the old and new guard played out in the background, the IRA needed money urgently. Bank and post office raids in the North only pulled in an estimated £500,000 a year. Other avenues had been closed off in the Republic, where large cash amounts were now transported under escort by the heavily armed Garda Task Force. Since the IRA's General Army Orders forbade any military action against the security forces in the Republic, security vans were, in effect, ruled off bounds.

Instead of hold-ups, which had a high risk factor, the IRA took to extorting the money from banks and business people by carrying out low-key kidnappings. Typically, a group of armed and masked men would break into the home of a businessman or bank manager in the middle of the night and hold his family hostage until the morning, when he was ordered to go the bank and withdraw money, generally between £10,000 and £50,000. There were fourteen such abduction cases reported to the Gardaí in 1982 and 1983, a number of which had paramilitary involvement. It was small change compared with the cost of keeping the war going. But one high profile kidnapping could bring in enough to cover the IRA's operating costs for a year. According to an intelligence source:

> The kidnappings were carried out by the Special Operations Team, which was a GHQ (General Headquarters) unit. The tactic at first was to raise low level finance by carrying out local kidnappings in the Republic. They weren't kidnappings in the sense that someone was taken hostage and a ransom was demanded. They would come in the middle of the night with guns, tie everyone in the house up and then send the husband down to the bank as soon as it opened in the morning. Many of these raids were never made public; they were never reported to the Gardaí. They raised quite a bit of money that went into the kitty. But around the time of the Shergar kidnapping, their finances were at such a low ebb they had to pull off a big one.

According to Sean O'Callaghan, the senior IRA informer, the idea of taking the racehorse came from Kevin Mallon, believed to be the organisation's head of operations at the time. A former bookies clerk, he was interested in racing and would have known how much Shergar was worth to his owners. A number of Volunteers were seconded from Southern Command to the shadowy Special Operations Unit that was to carry out the job.

The team that took the horse, O'Callaghan claimed, included Nicky Kehoe, the current Sinn Féin Dublin Councillor, Gerry Fitzgerald and the guts of the gang arrested during a shootout in County Wicklow later that year.

❖❖❖

Jimmy Fitzgerald dialled his boss's number as quickly as his trembling fingers allowed. 'There's a terrible thing after happening,' he said. Drion looked at the clock beside his bed. It was 1am. 'Shergar's been taken,' Fitzgerald said. Anxious not to wake his wife, Drion got out of bed and went downstairs to continue the call. Fitzgerald told him what had happened. Instead of phoning the Gardaí, Drion tried to contact the Aga Khan. He couldn't get him at his home in Sardinia and failed to get through to his executive secretary in Paris. Eventually, he tracked him down in Switzerland, where he was enjoying a skiing holiday in St Moritz. He told him the horse had been taken and the Aga Khan instructed him to go to the stallion box to check out Fitzgerald's story for himself. When he hung up, Drion phoned Stan Cosgrove, Shergar's vet, to tell him the news. 'I thought it was a joke,' Cosgrove remembers.

Cosgrove, who was also a shareholder in the horse, got dressed and drove the five miles from his home in Kildare to Drion's house at Sheshoon, the stud where Shergar was born. They drove from there to Ballymany, where they spent some minutes staring into the stallion's empty stall in silent disbelief. His nerves frayed, Fitzgerald told them the story again, almost without pausing for breath. He begged them not to phone the Gardaí in case the gang returned for his family. They decided to find out first what the Aga Khan wanted them to do. They went back to Drion's house and phoned him to confirm Fitzgerald's story. 'My God,' he said. 'This is terrible.'

The Aga Khan said he wanted the matter handled at the highest level. Drion made a pot of tea and he and Cosgrove sat in the kitchen, considering whom to phone. Drion decided to call Paddy McGrath, the chairman of the Irish Racing Board and a former TD, who was also a shareholder in the horse. His number was ex-directory so Cosgrove phoned a mutual friend, Sean Berry, who was general manager of the Irish Thoroughbred Breeders Association. It was now 3.30am and the Gardaí had still not been informed. Cosgrove apologised for phoning at such a late hour, but said that something serious had happened which he would soon read about in the newspapers. Berry gave him McGrath's number and went back to sleep. Fifteen minutes later, Cosgrove phoned back, unable to reach McGrath at his home. He told Berry what had happened at Ballymany Stud. 'In my business,' Berry wrote in his diary, 'it was the equivalent of the director of the Louvre being telephoned to say that the *Mona Lisa* had been stolen. Or dragging President Reagan out of bed and telling him that a Russian tank had been seen driving up Wall Street.'

Berry drove to Sheshoon and joined Drion and Cosgrove in the kitchen. Berry was a friend of Alan Dukes, the minister for finance, who lived nearby. They decided to call him. Dukes recalls:

I'd gone to bed early because I was presenting the Budget the next day. It was my first. I wanted a clear head so I decided to get a good sleep. In the middle of the night the phone rang. It was Sean. I was still asleep when I answered it, but I woke up pretty sharply when I heard what had happened. I said, 'Kidnapped? Are you sure?' Sean said he was. I asked him who would have kidnapped him, and he said he'd no idea. I asked him were the police there, and he said they hadn't called them yet. I said, 'You have to ring the police.'

It was only then, some time after 4am on Wednesday, more than seven hours after the horse had been taken, that the Gardaí were contacted. The call was made to Detective Inspector Senan Keogh, who lived nearby. He phoned Chief Superintendent James Murphy, who would lead what was to become the biggest search operation ever undertaken in the country.

Senior Gardaí were furious about the delay in phoning them, which cost them valuable search time. Ballymany was on the edge of the Curragh, home to the biggest concentration of army personnel in the country. Had the Gardaí been notified earlier, roadblocks with checkpoints could have been set up and the police on the other side of the border alerted. But by the time the authorities were told about the kidnapping, the horse could have been anywhere in the country. The Aga Khan's demand that Drion report the case to some unspecified higher authority seriously reduced the chances of finding Shergar. Stan Cosgrove admits that they made a mistake:

I suppose it was because the Aga Khan was like a statesman. This is
how he did business. If he had a problem, he didn't go calling the
cops. He called heads of State.

Three-and-a-quarter hours after Shergar was taken from
Ballymany, two Gardaí from Castleblaney, County Monaghan, were parked on a minor road about 300 yards from
the border, close to Ballynacarry Bridge. At 12.15am, a car
towing a horsebox passed them, heading in the direction of
Cullaville, a village across the border in County Armagh.
The dark brown car and the horsebox with its aluminium
roof and two wheels on either side tallied with the description of the Hillman Hunter and Pat Kelly's stolen horsebox.
This might have been the most important lead in the case
but the Gardaí didn't even know that Shergar was missing.

The operation had been expertly planned and brilliantly
executed. The timing of the kidnapping, just seven days
short of the start of the breeding season, was intended to put
pressure on the Aga Khan to pay up quickly and without
involving the Gardaí. The date itself was almost certainly
deliberately chosen. It was the night of the February bloodstock sale at Goffs, just fifteen miles up the N7, so the sight
of a car pulling a horsebox on the back roads in Kildare in
the late hours would have struck no one as suspicious.

The IRA were hitting a soft target. Security at Ballymany
was shockingly lax, as it was at many other studs. Racing
stables tended to be better protected, to stop horses being
drugged or nobbled before races. In 1981, Vincent O'Brien's
million pound Derby favourite, *Storm Bird*, was viciously
attacked in his stable at Ballydoyle, County Tipperary,

having its mane and tail hacked off. It ended the horse's career. Alarm systems, close circuit television and security guards became regular features of most racing yards after that. But, for whatever reason, once a racehorse retired and became a £10m asset with a £3m a year turnover, security became less of an issue. The main gates to Ballymany were unlocked. The alarm system hadn't been operating properly for some time. The closed circuit camera in the stallion box was only linked to two monitors, one in Fitzgerald's kitchen, the other in his bedroom, their function being to alert him if a horse had somehow injured itself in its stall.

Jonathan Irwin, who was then the manager of Goffs, remembers visiting Ballymany just before the kidnapping with a member of the Shergar syndicate, who wanted to see the horse up close for the first time:

> We walked into the stallion barns, identified Shergar, opened the door and stood in the box with him. It was about ten days before he was gone. One of the most valuable horses in the world and there was nothing to stop us taking him. In fairness, I don't think any of us would ever have believed that someone would want to kidnap a horse. But at the same time you had to do something to ensure headbangers or kids didn't get in.

By the time the Gardaí were on the case, the missing horse could have been anywhere, and the scattergun pattern of the searches that followed reflected this. In the beginning, the hunt centred on the border counties, but within days the Gardaí were looking in Kilkenny, Mayo, Kerry and Galway, and were even acting on the advice of clairvoyants and seers. On one occasion, the focus of the search switched to

Tynagh, after a British psychic claimed there were strong spiritual vibes emanating from the area.

The Government decided that there should be no deal with the kidnappers. The Taoiseach, Garret FitzGerald, asked the Gardaí to prevent any ransom being handed over.

> I don't recall whether there was any specific intelligence that the IRA were attempting to re-arm or that they were trying to get their hands on surface to air missiles. But it was clear that the money was to be put to use in the business of killing people. And what we wanted to make clear at the time was that the payment of any ransom to the Provisional IRA would lead directly to the loss of more innocent lives. We were one with the Gardaí on that point, that we had an active role to play in stopping terrorists getting their hands on money.

The worldwide publicity generated by the story could have had disastrous consequences for Ireland's burgeoning bloodstock industry. When Charles Haughey was Taoiseach he had introduced generous tax allowances to encourage people like the Aga Khan to base their operations in Ireland. It had worked. The breeding sector employed 20,000 people and was worth tens of millions of pounds to the economy every year. There were fears that the major breeders, especially the Arabs, who'd been enticed to Ireland from Britain, would pack up and leave. Jonathan Irwin recalls:

> This came at a time when English people would tell you on the best authority that the breeders and stud farmers here were already under threat from the IRA and were paying them some sort of protection money.

Nevertheless, Irwin was one of several leading figures in the breeding industry who offered to pay what he called 'a reward for information', but was really a ransom by another name. He says that his priority at the time was saving the horse's life, not catching criminals.

> It was done with the best of intentions, but looking back now, it wasn't the correct thing to do. I thought at the time that if they put a bullet in Shergar's head and he was found in a ditch somewhere it could have a knock-on effect that would hurt the thoroughbred industry in this country. My mistake was looking at it from that very narrow perspective. The man with all the hair – John McCrirrick – he lacerated me, said how dare we succumb to kidnappers and offer them money, and I understand his line of thought now because it's clear what the money would have been spent on. At the time, all that was important to us was getting the horse back. Nowadays I suppose you'd say what we were offering was blood money.

He wasn't the only who got carried away by his desire to get the horse back safely. Berry, a retired army captain, put aside his own personal loathing of the IRA to offer himself as a mediator between the kidnappers and the horse's owners. 'I don't think the Irish mentality would lend itself to doing anything to harm a horse,' he said at the time. His naivety embarrasses him now. Seven months earlier, on 20 July 1982, the IRA had detonated two nailbombs in Hyde and Regent's Park in London just before the changing of the guard at Horseguards' Parade. Eleven soldiers were killed, but it was the image of seven slaughtered horses that seemed to cause most outrage. Berry recalls:

I said at the time that I didn't think that even the IRA would shoot a horse. But of course that was wishful thinking.

❖❖❖

Except for the description of the three men offered by the Cullens, the Gardaí had very little to go on. Jimmy Fitzgerald, the only witness to the theft of the horse, was too traumatised by the experience to be of any help. Chief Superintendent Murphy didn't cut the figure of a dynamic criminal investigator. His mellow, laid-back nature and omnipresent trilby contributed to the 'Inspector Clouseau' caricature the press made of him. But when it came to old-fashioned, gumboot police work, 'Jazzer' – as he was known to his friends – was one of the best. He was born in Westclave, County Clare, and grew up on the family farm. Emigration was what passed for career ambition among young men of his generation and, like his friends, he'd made up his mind to leave when he saw an ad in the local newspaper. 'Become a policeman,' it said. He sat the exam without telling his parents, and passed. His first arrest, he once recalled, came at the end of a pushbike chase, when he caught up with a burglar by ramming him against a wall. That was in the early 1950s. Crime had indeed grown in sophistication over the following thirty years.

But Murphy had earned his stripes. He was the Garda who put Rose Dugdale's name to the Beit robbery in Russborough, and he was part of the team that tracked Eddie Gallagher and Marion Coyle to Monasterevin during the Tiede Herrema kidnapping. Lent was the time of year when he normally quit smoking. By the time Easter came around in 1983 he'd worried himself into a thirty-Major-a-day habit.

❖❖❖

At 1am on Thursday, 10 February, an anonymous caller to a Belfast paper, the *News Letter*, demanded that three British racing journalists – Derek Thompson, Lord John Oaksey of the *Sunday Telegraph* and Peter Camplin of the *Sun* – travel to Belfast to act as intermediaries in exchanging the money for the horse. Their instructions were to go to the Forum Hotel – now named the Europa – in the city centre to receive further orders.

Derek Thompson, a racing commentator with Thames Television, was woken from his sleep by the phone ringing. He presumed it was the 7.30am alarm call he'd ordered from reception. He answered and asked what time it was. A voice said it was 1.45am. He remembers:

> I asked him what the hell he thought he was doing, phoning me at that hour of the morning. He said he was from the Press Association in London and he was calling to tell me that Shergar's kidnappers had named me as one of the three journalists they wanted to act as mediators in the ransom exchange. Of course I said, 'You're drunk. On your bike,' and put the phone down. But he rang back a few seconds later and managed to persuade me it was genuine. By the time I got up, it was all over the news.

Thompson met up with Oaksey and Camplin and the three flew to Belfast that morning and caught a taxi to the Forum hotel. When they arrived, the place was swarming with pressmen. Within minutes, Thompson was paged and told there was a phone call. He picked it up in the foyer. A man with a southern accent, who called himself 'Arkle', told him to contact Judy Maxwell, the wife of Jeremy Maxwell, the horse trainer from County Down. Thomspon dialled the Maxwell home and an RUC officer answered the phone.

The Maxwells had been drawn into the plot earlier in the day, when they received three calls from what Judy described as a 'very rational, well-spoken man,' who again referred to himself as *Arkle*. He said they had been chosen as intermediaries for the handover of the ransom money for Shergar and to expect three English visitors some time in the afternoon. The RUC were called and they had an extra line installed in the house to ensure the phone was never engaged. Thompson, Oaksey and Camplin were told to make their way to Maxwell's 120-acre farm in Ballee, just outside Ardglass, an hour's drive from the centre of Belfast. 'But first we had to shake off this huge pack of journalists,' recalls Thompson.

> There must have been dozens of them there. They were all looking for a story, and at that point we were the story. But we couldn't arrive at the Maxwells' place with this huge posse following us, so the hotel's head of security took us down in an elevator, through the kitchen, out the back door and into a waiting car. It took us just over sixty minutes to get there. Once we got out of Belfast it was all countryside, quiet, narrow country roads. I was very frightened at this point and I presume John and Peter were. This was Northern Ireland in 1983 and you really had to think that anything could happen to us. So about a mile from the Maxwells, five men with machine guns, and their faces covered, stood out in middle of the road, telling us to stop. I wound the window down, terrified at this point, and he asked me was I Derek Thompson. I said I was. It

turned out they were the police, but they were all in plain clothes. He told me to go on up to the house, they were waiting for us.

Peter, John and I sat with the Maxwells and two police officers in the living room, drinking tea and waiting for the phone to ring. He called at 8.30 that night. I answered the phone. He said he was changing his name from 'Arkle' to 'Ekbalco', another famous race-horse. He said the ransom was £40,000, which, looking back, does seem very low, given the amount of planning that went into taking the horse and what he was worth to his owners alive. He said he wanted it publicised on the BBC.

The size of the ransom demanded should have alerted them straight away to the fact that it was a hoax. A post office robbery would have yielded more money.

Thompson phoned Ballymany to tell Drion about the demand, but Drion said he wasn't dealing with the matter. Having no faith in the Gardaí, the Aga Khan had hired David Watson, a former British army intelligence expert, who now ran a private security firm, to try to recover the horse. Thompson was told to phone Watson, who seemed unimpressed by what he had to say. Watson thought it sounded like a hoax. Thompson asked him to let the Aga Khan know, nonetheless, and to have him phone the house in Ballee. Watson said he couldn't promise anything. Oaksey and Camplin were inclined to agree with the Aga Khan's man, and they returned to the Forum, convinced they'd been had. Thompson remained in the house.

At half-ten that night the phone rang again. Jeremy Maxwell answered it this time. A woman caller said she had the Aga Khan on the line and she asked him to hold. He handed the phone to me.

Now, I'd interviewed the Aga Khan many times before at various race meetings and he had a very distinctive deep voice, and to me this was definitely him. He asked what the demand was and I told him it was £40,000. He said he'd call back. So, half an hour later, he rang back and he said, 'Proceed, we'll pay'. So I phoned the BBC, as the earlier caller had demanded, told them the news, and just before closedown they reported in a newsflash that the Aga Khan had agreed to hand over a £40,000 ransom for the kidnapped Derby winner, Shergar.

But something just didn't sit right with me. The conversation with the Aga Khan had been recorded and I remember sitting up into the small hours of the morning, listening to the tape over and over again, scrutinising his voice, his pronunciation of various words, the consistency in his tone, the inflections in his voice. And then I heard it. At the end of one of his sentences he said, 'You know,' which is something he would never have said. I realised then, to my utter horror, that I'd been duped. I stayed that night with the Maxwells, but I didn't sleep. At seven o'clock in the morning, 'Ekbalco', who'd now reverted to calling himself 'Arkle', phoned to say the horse had had an accident and had to be put down. I never did find out whether it was just some idiot's idea of a practical joke, or whether it was someone trying to divert attention away from the real negotiations.

Dave Watson had very good reason not to be excited by the story. Unbeknown to Thompson, or to the rest of the media, the IRA had actually been talking to the Aga Khan's people about Shergar's ransom since the day after the horse was taken. Early on Wednesday morning, 9th February, Ghislain Drion, the Ballymany manager, went to the

Fitzgerald home to see how Jimmy and the rest of the family were bearing up. While he was out, one of the kidnap gang phoned his house. Drion's wife said he was at Ballymany and suggested he try him at work. The caller did not ring the office straight away, but, for reasons that may have been significant, phoned in the middle of the afternoon, at around 3.45pm. Drion was away from his desk. When he phoned back again, twenty minutes later, he sounded agitated and angry.

The call was secretly recorded by Watson and the transcripts subsequently released by the Aga Khan's office. The kidnapper's annoyance, combined with Drion's halting English and apparent efforts to draw out the conversation to allow time for the call to be traced, lend a darkly comic twist to the conversation that followed:

Drion: 'allo, yes?

Kidnapper: Have you got … This is King Neptune.

Drion: Oo la la! Yes, oo la … You are very far away.

Kidnapper: Yes.

Drion: Could you repeat?

Kidnapper: No, I will repeat nothing. You will listen.

Drion: Yes.

Kidnapper: Have you got two million English pounds in twenties, fifties and one hundred bills, in used notes.

Drion: Oo la la … 'ave you got two hundred?

Kidnapper: Do not waste time!

Drion: Sorry?

Kidnapper: Do not waste time!

Drion: Do you not what?

Kidnapper: Do not waste time!

Drion: Waystime? What does that mean?

Frustrated, the caller hung up. When he rang back, at 5.45pm, he still hadn't calmed down.

Drion: 'allo, yes?

Kidnapper: No shit this time!

Drion: Yes.

Kidnapper: What I want from you–

Drion: Speak slowly if you want, I want I hear you and understand you, speak very slowly and clearly.

Kidnapper: I want a phone number in France.

Drion: Yes.

Kidnapper: Where I can contact you. I want it now.

Drion: In France? But I am in Ireland now.

Kidnapper: Don't give me any shit!

Drion: But you want a phone number where you can contact me in France?

Kidnapper: That's right. I want it now.

Drion: But I am living in Ireland.

Kidnapper: (after a long pause) I am going to hang up unless you start co-operating.

Drion: I can give you a phone number, yes?

Kidnapper: Now!

Drion: Let me think, eh … 'allo?

Kidnapper: Go ahead.

Drion: Eh … see, I am living in Ireland, yeah?

Kidnapper: I am hanging up in exactly sixty seconds, and your horse will be dead.

Drion gave him the telephone number of a friend in France.

Kidnapper: What part of France is that?

Drion: That's Paris.

Kidnapper: Okay. You be there at twelve o'clock tomorrow with two million English pounds.

Drion: That's impossible.

Kidnapper: Large denominations.

Drion: That's impossible because the Aer Lingus–

The caller hung up.

❖❖❖

It is unlikely that Kevin Mallon would have overlooked the fact that the Aga Khan owned only seven of the forty shares in the horse. He'd cashed in most of his interest in Shergar, and the value of his remaining shares was less than the £2m the IRA were demanding. To complicate matters, many of the shareholders in the horse had not purchased their £250,000 stakes outright, but had formed sub-syndicates with other investors. As many as a hundred different people may have owned a piece of Shergar. But the IRA didn't expect to have to deal with a whole democracy of owners. They figured the Aga Khan, who was worth an estimated £2 billion, loved the horse so much that he'd pay. Instead, the complex issue of the horse's ownership was used to stretch the negotiations to frustrate the kidnappers who, it was hoped, would leave the animal in a field somewhere. But the Aga Khan was prepared to see the horse killed rather than give in to the IRA.

According to Jonathan Irwin, who was a friend of his:

> He was absolutely adamant that he wouldn't hand over a penny.
> His attitude was: 'I'm not dealing with scum like you, if you can go
> low enough to steal a horse.' What you have to remember is that he
> was brought up in a world where he was always under threat of
> being kidnapped himself; right from the time he was a child. He
> lived a lot around Sardinia, which put him within easy reach of the
> Italian mafia. He was the head of a Muslim sect and a sworn enemy
> of Gaddafi. So I think he was somewhat well equipped to deal with
> situations like this. They picked the wrong man.

It is possible that Shergar was already dead by the time
Drion spoke to one of the kidnappers. Sean O'Callaghan,
former head of the IRA's Southern Command, who turned
informer, later claimed that a man who was supposed to
have experience of looking after horses was put in charge of
the animal. But the man had never handled an animal as
highly strung as a thoroughbred racehorse. Very soon after
the kidnapping, he claimed, Shergar threw himself into a
frenzy in the horsebox, damaged his leg and had to be shot.
It's not unreasonable to speculate that this may have
accounted for the long delay between the first call to Drion's
home early on Wednesday morning and the call to his work
number in the middle of the afternoon. According to a British intelligence source:

> The guy who'd been enlisted as a so-called expert in dealing with
> horses panicked when he couldn't control him. They just got scared
> and took the easy option, which was to snot him. But they tried to
> extort the money out of the owners anyway.

❖❖❖

Meanwhile, as the temperature plummeted and the ground hardenened, the Gardaí and the RUC, in a joint operation, searched farms, outbuildings, derelicts sites and stables along the border between South Armagh and Monaghan. But the hunt for the horse was going nowhere, frustrated by cranks and hoaxers who were drawn to the story like no other case the Gardaí had known. Mallon's belief that people would be ambivalent towards a kidnapping in which there was no grieving wife, mother or children was justified. The missing horse became a joke. Thousands of Garda man-hours were spent chasing up false leads. On Thursday, two days after the kidnapping, an anonymous caller to the *Drogheda Independent* said that the horse's head had been dumped on a farm in Togher, County Louth. Sean Berry had a call to say the horse was dead and had been thrown into a disused mine shaft in Silvermines, County Tipperary. Another caller told the Gardaí that the horse was within two miles of Ballymany. When the Gardaí and soldiers had spent two days scouring farmland and fields that had already been searched, the man rang back and repeated that Shergar was within two miles of the stud. When he was asked how he knew, he said, 'Sure he'd never get more than a mile and two furlongs, that one.'

Racing commentator Micheál O'Hehir received a call on Thursday, two days after the kidnapping, telling him to go to a pub on Parnell Street in Dublin city centre if he was interested in saving the horse's life. He did as instructed and nothing happened. A week later, on Valentine's night, the same man called again to say that Shergar was dead. If O'Hehir went to Davy and Phelan's pub in Blanchardstown in Dublin that night, he would be told where the body could be found. He duly went, and again no one approached him.

The difficulty for the Gardaí was that chasing up bogus leads meant directing their search efforts away from the border, the north midlands and the north west, the strong republican areas where they believed the horse was most likely to be found. Other, well-intentioned callers switched the attention of the Gardaí to Bunclody in County Wexford and an area east of the Corrib in County Galway. A farmer in County Clare was convinced that a stallion standing in a field next to his was Shergar. It wasn't.

The press, particularly the large contingent of British journalists, grew bored with the lack of hard news coming from the daily Garda news conferences in Newbridge. The newspapers filled the vacuum with fanciful stories speculating about what had happened to the horse. Cranks were given credence. Crackpot ideas were posited as theories. A clairvoyant said she saw Shergar in a dream, looking sad and distressed in the hold of a cargo ship bound for the Middle East. An anonymous caller to a British newspaper claimed he'd made the transportation arrangements to ship the horse to an unnamed Arab country, prompting speculation that the IRA had stolen the horse for Colonel Gaddafi as repayment for the arms he sent them in 1972. Other enemies of the Aga Khan were shaken down and asked if they hated him enough to take his horse.

The *Sun* claimed to have spoken to a member of the kidnap gang, who said that the horse had been smuggled to a farm in the south of France, where he would secretly sire a whole generation of great racehorses. It was an unlikely story. Shipping thoroughbred horses out of Ireland was a far from routine procedure, involving veterinary inspections, paperwork that had to be signed by the Department of Agriculture, and a raft of documents, including the horse's passport and a covering certificate. Not to mention the highly sophisticated blood-grouping checks on foals that a rogue breeder would have to get around.

Like Chief Superintendent Murphy, Drion was spending sixteen hours of every day at his desk, his phone ringing off the hook. As a reminder of how much money hung on Shergar's safe return, the first brood mares due to be covered by the stallion began arriving at Ballymany, their owners as anxious as anyone to know what was happening.

❖❖❖

Aware that the Gardaí would be trying to frustrate any ransom hand-over attempts, the IRA had decided not to conduct the negotiations in Ireland and they wanted Drion in Paris to stop the talks being monitored. But the Aga Khan told him to stay in Dublin, and instead chose a friend in Paris, whom he used as a third party negotiator in business deals, to talk to the kidnappers. While he had no intention of paying the IRA anything, he believed that a skilled negotiator could get them to see that their demands were futile and persuade them to let the horse go. On Thursday, arrangements were made to reroute the calls from the number Drion had given the IRA to the home of the Aga Khan's *chargé d'affaires* in Paris. The Gardaí knew about the negotiations from a wiretap on the phone at Ballymany, and told the Aga Khan's office they wanted a Garda present. He had no objections, and a murder squad detective who happened to be in Paris was sent to the home of the *chargé d'affaires* to listen in on the conversations.

The plan hit an immediate hitch. There was a delay in rerouting the calls to the new number, and on Thursday afternoon, when the kidnappers phoned the number that Drion gave them, there was no reply. The same man Drion had earlier spoken to phoned Ballymany and told his secretary that unless he got a response from the number by 9pm, they would never see the horse again. He warned that the Aga Khan's other interests in Ireland, France and America would be targeted next. At 9pm – exactly forty-eight hours since the horse was taken – he called the number again from a public payphone somewhere in Ireland. This time the transfer worked. The conversation, which was again recorded by Watson, was interrupted by repeated pips as the caller fed money into the phone to keep the call going.

Negotiator: Hello (pips). Hello (pips). Hello.

Kidnapper: Hello.

Negotiator: Hello.

Kidnapper: Drion?

Negotiator: Hello. No, it's not Drion. I am an employee of the company.

Kidnapper: Okay. This is King Neptune.

Negotiator: Yes.

Kidnapper: Have you got the money?

Negotiator: No.

Kidnapper: You haven't got the money?

Negotiator: No, we can't ... I mean there is about thirty-five share-holders on that, on that, on that thing ... (pips) ... hello.

Kidnapper: When will you have the money?

Negotiator: We have to have the agreement of the shareholders. We have to have proof that the horse–

Kidnapper: When? When? When? You are wasting time!

Negotiator: We have to have proof that the horse is alive.

Kidnapper: Listen ... (pips)...

Negotiator: Hello.

Kidnapper: Yes.

Negotiator: We have had many calls with many demands. We have no proof that you are the person holding the horse.

Kidnapper: We gave a codename when we took the horse.

Negotiator: The codename is in the press ... (pips)

Kidnapper: Listen, you obviously don't know the codename we are giving. You obviously are not the negotiator.

Negotiator: I got the name you have just mentioned now.

Kidnapper: Yes, that's the only one we have ever used.

Negotiator: Yes, this has now been in the press. Some newspapers have published that.

Kidnapper: Well, listen as ... like this. We have the horse and if you don't leave the money at that address, at that phone number, tomorrow night at nine o'clock, there's no more horse, okay?

Negotiator: We can't accept this. The shareholders will not accept ... the shareholders have to have proof definitely. There are thirty-five people.

Kidnapper: Proof that we have the horse?

Negotiator: Yes, and that it is alive.

Kidnapper: And that it's alive?

Negotiator: And that it is not harmed.

Kidnapper: Okay. You stay ... (pips)

Negotiator: Hello.

Kidnapper: You stay at that number. Okay?

Negotiator: Yes. What?

Kidnapper: You will remain at that number and we will give you proof ... (pips)

Negotiator: When? When will you give proof?

Kidnapper: We will give you proof whenever it is convenient to get proof, which could be today or it could be a week, but we will give you proof. So you stay at that number.

Negotiator: At this number?

Kidnapper: And whenever you get the proof, we want the money ... (pips)

Negotiator: We have to obtain an agreement–

Kidnapper: Whenever you get the proof, we want the money within three hours or the horse is dead. Goodbye.

Negotiator: Goodbye.

The Aga Khan's man was bluffing when he said that the codeword had been leaked to the press. Not one Irish or British newspaper made reference to 'King Neptune' in the days after the kidnapping. But the ruse bought him time. The gang turned its attention to devising a way of getting a photograph of Shergar to his owners to prove he was still alive. At 10pm on Friday night the caller phoned back, this time from a private phone:

Kidnapper: We have your proof. Have you got our money?

Negotiator: I don't have the money. I'm waiting for the proof.

Kidnapper: You're waiting for the proof?

Negotiator: Yes, because yes, we have heard from the news–

Kidnapper: You better have the money.

Negotiator: Sorry?

Kidnapper: You better have the money three hours after we give you the proof. Okay?

Negotiator: I have to first have the agreement from the shareholders. And you have heard the news in the press that the horse is dead?

Kidnapper: The news ... the news in the press is shite. We'll give you proof that the horse is alive.

Negotiator: Okay.

Kidnapper: Shut it off and listen for a minute.

Negotiator: Yes.

Kidnapper: What I want you to do is to get a person in Ireland who is not associated with the stuff or is not known by the police.

Negotiator: Yes.

Kidnapper: Tomorrow morning at nine o'clock in the Crofton Airport Hotel, Dublin ...

Negotiator: Airport hotel?

Kidnapper: Yes.

Negotiator: Crossing Airport Hotel.

Kidnapper: Crofton! C-R-O-F-T-O-N.

Negotiator: Crofton Airport Hotel.

Kidnapper: Dublin.

Negotiator: Dublin.

Kidnapper: Yes.

Negotiator: Yes.

Kidnapper: Give me the name of the person you are going to send.

Negotiator: Yes. I have to ... I have to ask for advice. I have to ask who can go, because I don't have any idea.

Kidnapper: You don't have an idea who can go?

Negotiator: No. Not yet. I mean, you're talking me just now.

Kidnapper: Tell the person who goes ...

Negotiator: Yes.

Kidnapper: ... use the name 'Johnny Logan'.

Negotiator: Whose name?

Kidnapper: Johnny Logan.

Negotiator: Johnny Logan.

Kidnapper: And be there. Tell him to leave his name at the desk.

Negotiator: Leave his name at the desk.

Kidnapper: Leave his name. Leave the name 'Johnny Logan', at the desk.

Negotiator: Yes.

Kidnapper: He will be contacted. At the hotel tomorrow morning at nine o'clock.

Negotiator: The person who is going to go–

Kidnapper: Yes.

Negotiator: He ... not to be associated with the–

Kidnapper: The stud.

Negotiator: With the stud?

Kidnapper: Yes.

Negotiator: Yes.

Kidnapper: Police do not know. And there is to be no police involved whatsoever.

Negotiator: Yes.

Kidnapper: You understand then?

Negotiator: Yes, I understand. That's why you changed the number.

Kidnapper: That's okay.

Negotiator: Yes.

Kidnapper: Use that number all the time now.

Negotiator: Yes.

Kidnapper: I'll phone, day or night.

Negotiator: Yes.

Kidnapper: Okay. Make sure you have the money. He has the proof; we have the money three hours after–

Negotiator: Yes, but I can't organise the money for tomorrow and I don't know, what's the amount, what's–

Kidnapper: The amount is as specified.

Negotiator: Yes.

Kidnapper: Two million pounds.

Negotiator: Yes.

Kidnapper: In used English–

Negotiator: Currency. Yes.

Kidnapper: Of twenty pounds to one hundred pounds and–

Negotiator: And where?

Kidnapper: We will get on to you again about where.

Negotiator: Yes. But in Ireland?

Kidnapper: You get proof, you have the money.

Negotiator: Yes, but we can't–

Kidnapper: We will tell you exactly what to do with the money.

Negotiator: Yes.

Kidnapper: Okay, thank you.

The conversation was relayed back to Murphy, who realised, probably better than the Aga Khan's man, that time was running out for Shergar, if indeed he was still alive. The caller's anger was coming to boiling point, and it was clear that the IRA weren't going to let the horse go simply out of frustration.

It was Stan Cosgrove who was sent to the Crofton Airport Hotel just north of Dublin at nine o'clock on Saturday morning, a clear breach of the order that someone unconnected with the horse be involved in the pick-up. He went to reception, introduced himself as Johnny Logan – the name of Ireland's Eurovision Song Contest winner of the previous year – and asked if a package had been left for him. 'There was nothing there,' he recalls.

> I told the girl I was going to hang around, and I asked to be paged in the breakfast lounge if anything came in for me. I had a cup of tea. I must have waited half an hour and nothing arrived, not even a phonecall. So I went back out to reception and I left a number there where I could be contacted if anyone rang looking for a Johnny Logan.

But Cosgrove wasn't the only one at the Crofton Airport Hotel that morning. A number of plainclothes Gardaí, including Inspector Senan Keogh, were staking out the hotel, and they had been spotted.

After Cosgrove left, frustrated, the IRA's negotiator phoned the Crofton and was given the number at which Cosgrove had said he could be contacted. It was the telephone number for Ballymany Stud. He was furious. Oddly, although the IRA were aware that the Gardaí had laid a trap at the hotel, the caller who phoned the Aga Khan's man in Paris at 11.15am didn't seem to be aware of it:

> Kidnapper: Hello.
> Negotiator: Yes?
> Kidnapper: You were supposed to have someone at that hotel.

Negotiator: Yes, we have.

Kidnapper: You haven't.

Negotiator: Yes, we have.

Kidnapper: I'm after ringing the hotel.

Negotiator: Yes?

Kidnapper: And they gave me the number of the stud.

Negotiator: Did they?

Kidnapper: Yes.

Negotiator: I have no information–

Kidnapper: You had better find out.

Negotiator: Yes.

Kidnapper: You have one hour to have someone at the hotel, okay?

Negotiator: Yes.

Kidnapper: One hour.

Negotiator: Okay.

Kidnapper: ... (inaudible) should you break the ... and call the police, okay?

Negotiator: Okay.

Kidnapper: No authorities whatsoever.

Negotiator: Okay.

Kidnapper: It's very bad-looking that you had ... someone left the number of the stud. We told you ... hotel ... nothing to do with the stud. Do you understand that?

Negotiator: I understand that.

Kidnapper: Someone completely clean. You better get someone there in exactly one hour.

Negotiator: Okay, okay.

Kidnapper: Or you're never going to see the horse again.

Negotiator: Okay.

That weekend, the Irish Farmers Association organised a mass countrywide search of land and disused farm buildings in an effort to find the horse. More than half of the entire Garda force and the army were involved in the search. If Shergar was still alive, the IRA must have known they couldn't hide him for much longer.

At 3.15pm the caller phoned Paris again:

Kidnapper: Hello.

Negotiator: Hello.

Kidnapper: Hello.

Negotiator: Yes, hello.

Kidnapper: This is King Neptune.

Negotiator: Yes.

Kidnapper: Just listen. I want you to answer some questions.

Negotiator: Yes.

Kidnapper: Are you the man with the sole power to hand over the money?

Negotiator: No, the shareholders have to decide. I have to refer to the shareholders.

Kidnapper: You get the person who has the sole power to negotiate and hand over the money on that phone.

Negotiator: Yes.

Kidnapper: In five minutes' time.

Negotiator: I am the only one capable of being on that phone.

Kidnapper: Right, well, you get the full power to negotiate.

Negotiator: Yes.

Kidnapper: You get it. Will you have it in five minutes?

Negotiator: The money?

Kidnapper: The sole power to negotiate.

Negotiator: I can try to get it.

Kidnapper: You better get it. Unless the person with sole power to negotiate and hand over the money is on the phone in five minutes the whole deal is off.

Negotiator: Mmm ...

Kidnapper: You understand that?

Negotiator: Well ... er ... I understand that, but I have to, I have to contact the shareholders. I can't ... they have the sole authority because–

Kidnapper: How long will it take you to contact the shareholders?

Negotiator: Sorry?

Kidnapper: How long will it take you to contact the shareholders?

Negotiator: Thirty-five people and they are all in Ireland, most of them.

Kidnapper: Well, listen, you have exactly sixty minutes.

Negotiator: Yes.

Kidnapper: Sixty minutes.

Negotiator: Sixty minutes.

Kidnapper: To have the power to hand over that money and to negotiate. I'm fed up being messed around.

Negotiator: Em ...

Kidnapper: We're fed up being messed around.

Negotiator: You're fed up?

Kidnapper: Listen, don't get fucking smart. Just listen.

Negotiator: Yes.

Kidnapper: We're fed up being messed around.

Negotiator: Yes.

Kidnapper: Okay?

Negotiator: Okay.

Kidnapper: We know all you're doing is delaying us ...

Negotiator: No.

Kidnapper: The police will never get your horse back.

Negotiator: We believe that the horse is dead.

Kidnapper: Listen.

Negotiator: Yes.

Kidnapper: The proof that the horse is still alive has been ... is at this minute at the Rosnaree Hotel.

Negotiator: Yes.

Kidnapper: If you go to that hotel–

Negotiator: Yes.

Kidnapper: ... and you ask for an envelope left for Johnny Logan.

Negotiator: Yes.

Kidnapper: You have the proof that the horse is still alive and well.

Negotiator: Could you repeat the name of the hotel and the place?

Kidnapper: The Rosnaree Hotel.

Negotiator: Yes.

Kidnapper: On the main Dublin-Belfast road.

Negotiator: Dublin-Belfast road. Yes, okay. And the proof is there? Johnny Logan.

Kidnapper: Yes.

Negotiator: Okay, with the desk ... sorry?

Kidnapper: If you phone that message to Ireland ...

Negotiator: Yes.

Kidnapper: ... the Special Branch will get the proof and they will withhold the proof from the shareholders. You must understand that.

Negotiator: Yes.

Kidnapper: Okay?

Negotiator: Okay.

Kidnapper: I'll ring in one hour.

Negotiator: Yes.

Kidnapper: You–

Negotiator: ... should have the–

Kidnapper: ... the person there with the sole power to negotiate and hand over the money.

Negotiator: I will try to get this power myself.

Kidnapper: Yes and you've got one hour. That's the limit.

Negotiator: Yes.

Kidnapper: No more discussion. No more deals after one hour. Unless you have that power there's no more deals. You'll never see the horse again.

Negotiator: Yes, but we may have–

Kidnapper: Do you understand that?

Negotiator: Yes, but–

Kidnapper: Okay. One hour.

Negotiator: Yes, but we may have to ring back to Ireland ... Hello.

Kidnapper: It doesn't matter. You ring, but you have it done inside sixty minutes because we're fed up. You're only putting the horse in danger.

Negotiator: Yes, but–

Kidnapper: The longer we hold onto it, the longer, the more dangerous it becomes.

Negotiator: I understand this.

Kidnapper: The proof is at the hotel. I told you.

Negotiator: Yes, but I want to stress a point that the persons, the shareholders, may nominate someone in Ireland to have the power. In that case–

Kidnapper: ... his name and number.

Negotiator: I would, I would give you the name, the number and you can contact him.

Kidnapper: And we will be pulling him over to Paris with you.

Negotiator: Okay.

Kidnapper: We do not want to deal with people in Ireland.

Negotiator: You don't want to deal in Ireland?

Kidnapper: No.

Negotiator: But if this person is empowered in Ireland, what happens?

Kidnapper: If he is in Ireland, you have his name and address and phone number.

Negotiator: Yes.

Kidnapper: You ring and get him to Paris. You get him to Paris.

Negotiator: Okay.

Kidnapper: By next time I ring, you will have him there.

Negotiator: Okay.

Kidnapper: You have one hour to have a person there at that phone. We don't care how you do it.

Negotiator: Yes.

Kidnapper: You have a person there at that phone in one hour with total negotiating power.

Negotiator: Okay

Kidnapper: ... fed up!

Negotiator: Okay.

Kidnapper: Okay?

Negotiator: Okay, understood.

The caller was generous. He waited an hour-and-a-half before ringing back. But by then he knew the Gardaí had been at the Crofton Hotel that morning and that the demand for proof was a ruse to draw them out into the open. He rang Paris at 5pm:

Negotiator: Hello.

Kidnapper: Hello, this is King Neptune.

Negotiator: Hello, I can't hear you.

Kidnapper: Can you hear me?

Negotiator: Yes, I can hear you.

Kidnapper: This is King Neptune.

Negotiator: Yes.

Kidnapper: Have you the money?

Negotiator: I am presently trying to reach all the shareholders. I don't yet have the proof of the existence. I want them to accept the proof of the existence and nominate their representative. We are working on this – it is not ready yet.

Kidnapper: But you have got the proof, yes?

Negotiator: Sorry?

Kidnapper: Have you got the proof, yes?

Negotiator: We have gone for the proof but it is not back yet …

Kidnapper: … (interference)…

Negotiator: Hello? Hello? Hello?

Kidnapper: Hello, listen.

Negotiator: Yes.

Kidnapper: The proof is there.

Negotiator: Sorry?

Kidnapper: The proof is there.

Negotiator: Yes, we have sent someone.

Kidnapper: You can pick up the proof at any time.

Negotiator: Yes, someone … sorry?

Kidnapper: Listen …

Negotiator: Sorry? Sorry?

Kidnapper: Don't be holding me back.

Negotiator: Yes.

Kidnapper: You can pick up the proof at any time.

Negotiator: We have sent someone to pick up the proof.

Kidnapper: Now, you can get that at any time, right? Have you got the money ready now?

Negotiator: No, the money is not ready. I always told you–

Kidnapper: Listen.

Negotiator: Yes?

Kidnapper: If you don't have the money ready by tonight–

Negotiator: Sorry, I can't hear you.

Kidnapper: Why have you not got the money ready?

Negotiator: I told you, I have to have the agreement of the shareholders.

Kidnapper: That's bullshit. Okay, what I want to know: are you going to pay the money for the horse, yes or no?

Negotiator: We have to have the proof the horse is alive and has not been harmed, because we are not going to pay and the shareholders are not going to pay–

Kidnapper: Are they not going to pay up the money?

Negotiator: ... if the horse has been harmed. And they are not going to pay for a useless horse.

Kidnapper: Listen ...

Negotiator: They are certainly not going to pay for a useless horse, you can be sure of that ...

Kidnapper: Listen. Just you listen.

Negotiator: Yes.

Kidnapper: As we said, it will be only a matter of time until all the shareholders have it.

Negotiator: Yes.

Kidnapper: Okay. There is nothing now stopping you getting the money.

Negotiator: Yes.

Kidnapper: Now, are you willing to pay the amount specified?

Negotiator: We have to get the money, then we have to get the agreement of the shareholders.

Kidnapper: Listen, you're agreeing or you're not.

Negotiator: The shareholders–

Kidnapper: Are the shareholders going to pay the money, or are they not?

Negotiator: I don't know yet.

Kidnapper: Listen, I want that answer now, because if I don't get that answer, I'm taking it … I'm assuming that you are not going to pay the money, and then there is no point in us holding on to this horse any longer.

Negotiator: I can't make commitments and then not have the money. You see what I mean? I can't make the commitments for them.

Kidnapper: Is it the shareholders' intention to pay the money?

Negotiator: I don't know the intentions of the shareholders yet.

Kidnapper: Well, you better find them.

Negotiator: Yes.

Kidnapper: Get the intention of the shareholders, and the next time I call you, you better either tell me that you are going to pay the money and that you have it ready, or that you are not going to pay the money.

Negotiator: Yes, but tell me–

Kidnapper: You fully understand?

Negotiator: Yes.

Kidnapper: The next time I phone, I want–

Negotiator: When are you going to phone?

Kidnapper: I will phone very shortly.

Negotiator: Very shortly?

Kidnapper: Very shortly.

Negotiator: Leave me some time to do that.

Kidnapper: You better hurry yourself.

Negotiator: We are working on that.

Kidnapper: If we have to kill this horse, it'll be you that killed him.

Negotiator: Yes, but you will be responsible to your country for that.

Kidnapper: What?

Negotiator: You are going to damage the reputation of your country and its economy.

Kidnapper: Do you think I give a shit about it?

Negotiator: Oh, in that case that's another matter.

Kidnapper: That is another matter, right.

Negotiator: Right.

Kidnapper: All I'm interested in is getting that money. You're either willing to pay the money or not willing to pay the money.

Negotiator: Okay, I will convey this message immediately, but it takes me some time to get all these people.

Kidnapper: Listen, just let me make one more point to you.

Negotiator: Yes.

Kidnapper: You may not pay for this horse, but you will definitely pay for the next one when you see what we do to this horse. Do you understand that?

Negotiator: Yes, I do.

Kidnapper: Okay.

Negotiator: Thank you.

Kidnapper: When I ring back, I want–

Negotiator: When are you going to ring back?

Kidnapper: I will ring you back before the night is out.

Negotiator: Okay.

Kidnapper: And I want a definite answer as to whether you are willing to pay that money.

Negotiator: Okay, I will contact–

Kidnapper: ... willing to pay the money. You must have the money with you.

Negotiator: Yes.

Kidnapper: Do you understand that?

Negotiator: Yes, but it is Saturday. The banks are closed.

Kidnapper: I don't give two fucks!

Negotiator: I'm in France. If you want this money in France, if you want this money in France, I have to get this amount in sterling pounds in France.

Kidnapper: Listen.

Negotiator: Yes.

Kidnapper: You have had a lot of days and a lot of time to get the money.

Negotiator: Yes, but–

Kidnapper: So anything you're saying just now is bullshit, okay? If you really intend to pay the money for the horse, you will have it there.

Negotiator: I don't have it.

Kidnapper: In the bank.

Negotiator: I don't have it.

Kidnapper: You had better get it.

Negotiator: Yes, but now I don't have it.

Kidnapper: Fuck you. I want a commitment.

Negotiator: Okay.

Kidnapper: It matters nothing to me about the horse. You'll pay for the next horse.

Negotiator: Okay.

Kidnapper: Do the cops know that you are in contact with us?

Negotiator: I don't know.

Kidnapper: How come the hotel was full of cops this morning?

Negotiator: I don't know.

Kidnapper: Listen, if any of my people had been caught this morning, I would not only have killed the horse, but I would have killed you and everyone else I have been in contact with. Do you understand that?

Negotiator: I understand that.

Kidnapper: You better understand that.

Negotiator: Okay.

Kidnapper: Do you understand the kind of people you are dealing with?

Negotiator: Yes.

Kidnapper: Okay, when we say the horse is alive, it's alive.

Negotiator: Okay.

Kidnapper: And whenever we say it's dead, it will be dead.

Negotiator: Yes.

Kidnapper: If you are not willing to pay the money, forget about it. Just you say that.

Negotiator: Okay.

Kidnapper: But you had better have an answer for me this evening.

Negotiator: Okay.

Kidnapper: And if you are willing to pay the money, I'm sure that your very rich friends can get any bank to open up and give them that amount of money.

Negotiator: Okay.

Kidnapper: It's only a drop in the ocean.

Negotiator: I will convey that.

Kidnapper: Okay.

Negotiator: Okay.

Kidnapper: Just remember, you are not dealing with fools.

Negotiator: Okay.

Kidnapper: And if any of my people do get caught, you just look after yourself, son.

Negotiator: Okay.

Kidnapper: Okay.

Negotiator: Thank you.

Kidnapper: Right, I'll ring you back this evening.

Negotiator: Okay.

That afternoon, an envelope was left at the reception desk of the Rosnaree Hotel in Drogheda, County Louth for a Johnny Logan. It was collected by a Garda detective. Inside was a black and white Polaroid photograph featuring a close-up of Shergar's head and next to it a human hand pointing at the previous day's edition of the *Irish News*, a Belfast newspaper. Cosgrove was shown the photograph in Newbridge that night. He was more intimate with Shergar than anyone. He remembers:

> It was him alright. From the whites of his eyes and the marks on his face there was no doubt about it in my mind. It was definitely him, but you couldn't have told from the photograph whether he was alive or dead. His eyes were open, but horses often die with their eyes open. So he could easily have been dead and they set up the picture to make it look like he wasn't. It's possible.

Dead or not, the IRA had offered as much evidence as they were going to. The Aga Khan's man had done well to stall the kidnappers for three days, especially after the double-cross at the Crofton Hotel. The final call to Paris was made on Saturday night, at 10.40pm.

Kidnapper: Have you the money?

Negotiator: Mr Drion is not satisfied with the proof and I'm sure the shareholders will not be satisfied with it.

Kidnapper: You are not satisfied?

Negotiator: They need further proof.

Kidnapper: If you are not satisfied, that's it.

The caller put the phone down. If Shergar was still alive at that point, it's probable that he was shot shortly afterwards.

❖❖❖

On Sunday, 13 February 1983, Chief Superintendent Murphy, having been told about the abrupt end to the talks in Paris, expressed doubt in public for the first time about whether the horse was still alive. The press, unaware of the turn that events had taken, hung around Kildare for a few more weeks, waiting for a breakthrough. The British tabloids took their frustration out on Murphy, portraying him as a small-town policeman who was out of his depth in a case like this. He turned up at Monday's news conference to discover that the entire front row was wearing trilbies as an ironic tribute to him. It might explain his reluctance to talk about Shergar twenty years on. 'I retired from the Gardaí,' he says, 'and once I was out of it, I decided I wouldn't talk about it ever again.'

There were more twists in the story in the weeks that followed. On Tuesday, 15 February, a radio ham in Galway made a tuning error and intercepted a conversation between four men who appeared to be discussing transportation arrangements for a horse. The exchange was picked up on a frequency usually used by the police in England and seemed to involve two walkie-talkies and two fixed stations. The conversation was peppered with short, cryptic messages such as, 'Wendy is here now,' references to the road surface being 'very bad for the box,' and comments on other cars they saw on their route. Thirty Gardaí searched farms and outbuildings over a huge area between Cong and Moycullen as a result, but found nothing.

On the same day, in Dungannon, County Tyrone, Paddy McCann, a horseracing enthusiast, was walking his dog along Bush Road when he found a portion of a horse's hind leg, which had been hacked off below the knee. Though the hair was long and unkempt, he recognised the leg as belonging to a thoroughbred. The RUC sent it to Belfast for forensic testing but it didn't belong to the horse they were looking for. These types of stories kept Shergar's name in the news for months, and stories continued to surface suggesting that the horse was still alive. However, from their knowledge of the Paris negotiations, the only Shergar mystery that remained for the Gardaí four days into the kidnapping was where he had been put in the ground.

❖❖❖

The IRA didn't abandon their efforts to get paid. Four weeks after the final call to France, they launched what the Gardaí believe was a salvage operation, with the reward money put up by the Irish Thoroughbred Breeders Association as their target. Collecting meant maintaining the pretence that the horse was still alive. Sean Berry and Jonathan Irwin had gone on radio several times offering a substantial reward for the return of the horse. But, according to Berry, they were bluffing:

There was no money. The truth about it is there was never as much as twenty pounds. I was going around, with my neck on the block, saying there was £250,000 there if they would just give us the horse back. I didn't have that much money. And I'd no backing for it either, for what we were saying – none. I just got over-enthusiastic.

The IRA didn't know that. At 8.15pm on St Patrick's Day, a man phoned Berry's number and asked him to put a figure on the reward he was talking about on the radio. Berry told him, off the top of his head, that it was £100,000. The caller said it wasn't enough, then passed the phone on to another man, with 'a cultured Irish accent,' who said that if he could raise £250,000 then the negotiations could begin. Berry said he didn't foresee any difficulty finding that kind of money. Before he hung up, the caller said that in future he would use the codename 'Rugby'. Berry figured someone was doing his homework on him. He was fanatical about the game, having played it in school and in the army.

Berry had done peacekeeping duties in Palestine, India, Pakistan and Syria. He hated the IRA and agonised over what to do next. He wrote in his diary:

I asked myself why the hell I was doing all this in the first place, when the owners and guardians of the missing Shergar had been so lax in their security and so slow to move once the theft had been discovered. When half the nation seemed to regard the whole thing as 'a bit of a lark' on the part of the 'lads', whose activities are only too often looked upon with the misguided tolerance of the Irishman for the rebel, even when that rebel is trying to undermine and over-throw the lawfully elected government of their so-called 'beloved' country. Why was I taking upon myself the responsibility and danger of being the front man, when possibly the best odds I could hope for were a hiding to a bullet in the head?

In the end, Berry decided he would talk to them. With his permission, the Gardaí tapped his office and home tele-phone lines and offered to put up the ransom money as bait to draw the kidnappers out. Four nights later, on 21 March at 7.45pm, the caller rang back. 'Is the £250,000 okay?' he asked. Berry agreed that it could be raised. 'I'll be back shortly,' the caller said, and hung up. Three nights later he called again. 'Have you the money ready?' he asked. Berry hadn't slept well for a few days and by this time his temper was on a very short fuse. 'Listen,' he remembers shouting, 'I'm bloody fed up with your messing about. I can have the money in twenty-four hours, but I absolutely refused to dis-cuss the matter any further unless you first produce evi-dence that you have Shergar and that the horse is unharmed. Otherwise you are just wasting my time. So let me have the evidence or forget the whole deal. No more phone calls until then.' He slammed the phone down.

At that point the Gardaí were not only tapping his phone lines, they were literally living in his house. Berry and his wife had planned to take a two-week holiday in the Canary Islands. Seeing how stressed he was, Irwin told his friend to go, and offered to stand in for him on phone duty for a fort-night. The calls were rerouted to a special line installed in Irwin's home. For two weeks he sat by the phone and no one called. 'Except one afternoon,' Irwin recalls. 'This new phone they put in specially started ringing. I just froze and I looked at the Garda who was sitting there next to me. He said, "Are you going to answer it?" The adrenalin was pumping. I picked it up and said hello. And a voice said, "Is that McGrattan's hair salon?"'

On 10 April, Berry and his wife returned home. As the weeks passed, he began to forget all about Shergar. Then, on 2 May the caller rang again. He seemed to know Berry had been out of the country. His first words were, 'You're back.' He said he was introducing a new code – Fiat 127. It was the make of car that Berry's daughter, Vivienne, drove, and Berry took it as an implicit threat. The caller said: 'We want to meet up with you today. Go to the Hotel Keadeen now and await a phone call at 11am. You will be known as Mr Davies. We will ask for you by that name. If you're serious about this, don't blow it. We won't, but if you do you are putting your own neck in danger. Got that?' Then he hung up.

Berry phoned the Special Branch handler he'd been assigned, who told him to follow the caller's instructions and not to worry. The Gardaí would have him covered, he said. At 10.45am, he pulled into the forecourt of the Keadeen, just outside Newbridge, County Kildare. He knew the reception staff well and felt embarrassed at asking to be paged if anyone called for a Mr Davies. He spent ten or fifteen minutes waiting, during which time he became aware that a man on the other side of the foyer was staring at him. At 11am precisely the phone call came. The caller told him he would be collected at two o'clock the following day and taken to see the stallion. He had until then to get the £250,000 together. When he hung up, he noticed that the man who'd been staring at him was gone.

He talked to his handler, who told him to return to the hotel the following day. A radio-tracking device was fitted to his car by the Gardaí so they could follow his movements. Since Berry had no money with him, he was told to take a more adversarial line with the caller, demanding proof that he had the horse. The caller rang at 2pm and asked for Mr Davies. 'Are you ready to be picked up, and have you got the money,' the man asked. Berry launched into a tirade, which he recorded in his diary:

> No, I bloody well have not got the money, and I am not going any-
> where with you until you produce evidence of Shergar being alive.
> Do you think I am some sort of bloody fool to go off on an unknown
> chase with someone I have never met, with maybe nothing at the
> end of it but maybe a bullet in the head? You want two hostages by
> the sound of you – Shergar *and* me. If you have got him, let me have
> evidence of it. But you won't have me. It shouldn't be too hard for
> you to produce evidence and leave it somewhere, like here, for me
> to pick up. Then, if it can be verified satisfactorily, we will make the
> next move. You know where to find me, so it is easy for you to come
> across with evidence. But until you do, I am not having any more of
> this trailing around Kildare, answering unknown telephone callers,
> making a fool of myself and wasting my time.

Berry slammed down the phone. Then he left the hotel and drove to the carpark of Newbridge College to meet his handler. He told him he'd unfortunately lost his temper. A plainclothes detective who was in the reception area said that the same man who was watching Berry the previous day was watching him again, this time from behind a copy of the *Daily Telegraph*.

The caller didn't phone again until two days later, 5 May, at 8.30pm. He referred to Berry by his Christian name for the first time and playfully ticked him off over his attitude during the last call. Berry told him he had no plans to apologise, and that he should get off the line unless he had something constructive to say. 'Go into Kildare town,' the caller instructed. 'There are two telephone kiosks there, back to back. The phone numbers are 21368 and 21625. Go into one of the boxes and you will be called again later.'

Berry made the five-minute drive into town and found the two kiosks, which were outside the Garda station. Both were vacant. He went into one and picked up the receiver, but kept the receiver button pressed down with his finger, and stood there pretending to talk. An hour passed. The phone rang. 'About bloody time,' he snapped. 'What nonsense are you up to now? Come on, stop fucking me about. Let me have the proposition.' The caller told him to shut up and listen. 'We want to know,' he said, 'whether you are sure you could positively identify Shergar.'

Berry knew what Shergar looked like, but a horse's markings can easily be altered through dyeing, so Berry had taken the precaution of collecting a blood-typing kit from Wetherbys in case he was ever asked to identify him. 'I'm ninety per cent positive,' he responded. 'I would need to have a straight opportunity to examine him, with no interference, no messing about, no threats. And no money until identification was positive and the horse was found to be fit and well.' There was silence. 'Will you agree to my being picked up and taken to see the horse, without bringing any money?'

The caller said, 'If you do, you will have to remain where the horse is until the money is paid. A quarter of a million pounds. We are not going to let you go. We can't afford to do that, not once you have seen the stallion's hiding place. You realise that, don't you, Sean?'

Stan Cosgrove had offered to go along with him to identify the horse. Berry suggested his name. 'He is the obvious expert on the horse. Do you know Mr Cosgrove?' The caller said he did: 'As far as I know, it would be alright for him to come with you, but I'll check and call you again.'

He didn't call back. The kidnappers might have known that they were being lured into a trap, or perhaps it was just another of the many hoaxers who were drawn to the search for the horse. But there the trail of the men who stole Shergar went cold.

❖❖❖

The failure of the Shergar operation was disastrous for Mallon. At the time, his influence within the republican movement was waning as the Adams faction wrested control from the old traditionalists he was close to, like Ruairí Ó Brádaigh and Daithí Ó Connail. 'Mallon was in charge of the Shergar job, but within the IRA he was becoming an irrelevance really,' says an IRA source.

He was a dinosaur, a Fifties man who couldn't make the transition. He was Border Campaign. He couldn't see that the nature of the war was changing. I think the politicals, like Adams and McGuinness, were going to have to take him on eventually, but in the end they didn't need to. Shergar damaged his credibility. It was 1983 that really finished him.

There was one final ironic twist to the Shergar story. The kidnapping and killing of the horse didn't have the fatal consequences for the Irish bloodstock industry that Irwin and others predicted. In a perverse way it might have helped it. There is never a guarantee that a champion stallion's progeny will emulate their father's powess, and Shergar turned out to be a one-off. According to Irwin:

I have to say, long term, whoever did it, did the general stud book a great favour, because the one crop of horses that he did produce showed him to be an absolute, potentially disastrous stallion. Not one of his offspring turned out to be a great racehorse. He wasn't a good-looking horse and his foals were pretty unattractive. He was a freak really; you get them. They're what keep the sport challenging. They're what stop John Magnier and the Arabs from sewing it up between them. There'll always be some Mickey Mouse horse who comes along and, for no rhyme or reason, just runs. And that was Shergar. But he could have impregnated an awful lot of our mares with what I'd have to say now was a very poor genetic. I often think to myself, thank God he disappeared off the face of the planet.

CHAPTER TWO

Kidnapping by the Book
Lord and Lady Donoughmore

*'You had this unit driving around the Irish countryside with
this fucking book, a hardback,* The Stately Homes of Ireland, *and
they had it spread out on their laps. This is what they
were working from. Pictures of rich people's homes.'*
IRA source

At two o'clock on the afternoon of Tuesday, 4 June 1974, Joe
Phelan watched a blue Ford Cortina drive slowly past the
gate lodge of Knocklofty House, County Tipperary, where he
lived with his family. His father, Tom, had been chauffeur
and gunkeeper to Lord Donoughmore, the wealthy peer, for
more than thirty years. Knocklofty House was a twenty-four
bedroom, eighteenth-century stately home set on a 650-acre
estate a few miles from Clonmel. It was a tranquil, sparsely
populated area in the rolling foothills of the Comeragh and
Knockmealdown mountains, where outsiders tended to
stand out. The three men in the Cortina did. They were taking
everything in. When they saw that Joe had noticed them, they
turned their faces away and the car sped off.

❖❖❖

Taoiseach Liam Cosgrave was worried. He had been alerted by Garda intelligence that a group of extremists on the fringes of the Provisional IRA was planning a high profile kidnapping. Members of the Irish and British governments and their families had been identified as likely targets. Cosgrave himself, the minister for justice Paddy Cooney and the minister for foreign affairs Garret FitzGerald, were warned that they were most at risk.

Cosgrave regarded the IRA as a threat to democracy as well as to the State. When he received the kidnap warning he decided that there was only one way to deal with it. In the autumn of 1973, Cosgrave sat down with his Cabinet and made a death pact. The deal that he and his colleagues agreed on was that they were all expendable. If any one of them was taken hostage, there would be no bartering for his life. If a minister's wife or any member of his family was snatched, the minister would immediately resign from the government and no negotiations would be entered into with the kidnappers, even if it meant the murder of a loved one. According to Garret FitzGerald:

> The information we got was that a member of the Government could be kidnapped by some unnamed subversive group. Ministers didn't have a great deal of protection at the time. Our official Garda drivers carried guns, but if we left our cars their instructions were to remain with the cars. It appeared the guns were to protect the State cars rather than the ministers. It was very strange. So after we got this warning we all got two more armed guards, who escorted us in another car. I remember that around that time we also talked about it, this kidnapping threat. Because, while we now

felt a bit safer, we knew that our families were still quite open. So everyone in the Government sat down, and we agreed that if any of our wives or members of our families were taken hostage, then that person would resign from Cabinet and no concessions would be made.

The Cosgrave years were a time of uncertainty and fear in the Republic and marked a dramatic change in the security climate. The Dublin and Monaghan car bombings killed thirty-three people and brought the reality of the modern Troubles spilling across the border for the first time. The murder of Senator Billy Fox, the assassination of the British Ambassador to Ireland, Christopher Ewart Biggs, and a number of spectacular prison breaks and hijackings demonstrated the strength and ruthlessness of the resurgent IRA and created the sense of a country under siege. The organisation was openly flouting the authority of the State and Cosgrave felt the same pressure to deal with them as his father, William T Cosgrave, Ireland's first Taoiseach, did in 1922. Liam's response was a raft of new anti-terrorism laws, while the term 'subversives' became common coinage to describe republicans during the time of his Government.

To Paddy Cooney it was a seminal point in history. The IRA appeared to be operating with impunity within the Republic, and the Government had to show the force of its will. He remembers:

> Around that time – the Seventies – kidnapping, not just in Ireland, was a not uncommon terrorist tactic and it was agreed that it could not be rewarded, for to do so would be likely to increase its incidence, and the Government had to take the lead.

In fact, at that time the Provisional IRA – reborn out of the sectarian fighting that exploded in Belfast and Derry in the late 1960s – was opposed to kidnapping, though more for operational than ideological reasons. Taking a hostage was like poking a wasp's nest with a stick. The huge mobilisation of police and soldiers that inevitably followed led to safe houses being turned over and arms dumps being uncovered. The IRA knew that a kidnapping in the Republic would bring untold heat on the organisation, inviting the Government to introduce even more repressive security measures and laws, while alienating them from their silent sympathisers in the political establishment and the Gardaí. Many republicans already suspected that Cosgrave planned to introduce internment without trial in the Republic as a sop to Brian Faulkner, the leader of the new power-sharing executive in Northern Ireland. At the very least, they believed his hard-line law-and-order government would conduct a round-up of suspects and put them before the juryless Special Criminal Court on nebulous membership charges.

'The biggest issue we had with kidnappings was that they paralyse the whole country,' says one senior IRA figure from the time.

They put all kinds of things at risk – arms dumps, planned operations, safe houses. You're got guys on the run who are put at serious risk of capture because all of a sudden there's this heightened state of security. There's roadblocks, searches. It makes it impossible to operate. And it gives the police a perfect excuse to round republicans up. To go into their homes and tear them up. And they knew it

was inevitable they'd find stuff. The guards would use things like
that as an excuse for a huge intelligence-gathering exercise.

The intelligence supplied to Cosgrave about the kidnapping threat almost certainly referred to a small group of dissident IRA Volunteers who were operating around the border, carrying out bank raids and gun attacks from the relative sanctuary of the Republic. British Prime Minister Harold Wilson and the security forces in Northern Ireland had been putting pressure on Cosgrave for some months now to deal with them. And the Garda intelligence was well founded.

It was a time when emotions were running high among republicans because of the treatment of the Price sisters, and many were of the opinion that something drastic had to be done to save them. Marian and Dolours Price, two sisters who were members of the first Provisional IRA active service unit to bomb London, were on hunger strike in Brixton Prison, demanding to be allowed serve their sentences as political prisoners in Northern Ireland. They were being subjected to forced feeding, a cruel and draconian process that involved clamping the mouth with a metal device and inserting a tube down the oesophagus into the stomach.

❖❖❖

On 27 December 1973, a group of IRA Volunteers, acting without authorisation, kidnapped Thomas Niedermayer, the West German consul in Belfast, in the hope of exerting international pressure on the British to end the ordeal of the sisters. But the operation was badly botched. Niedermayer was the managing director of the successful Grundig plant in Dunmurry, which produced cassette recorders and was one of the biggest cross-community employers in the unemployment ghetto of Belfast. Two days after Christmas, one of his teenage daughters answered the door of their home to two young men who said they'd been involved in a minor accident with his car, which was parked outside the house. Niedermayer went outside to inspect the damage, and his family never saw him again. He was forced into the back of a car and driven the short distance to a house in Hillhead Crescent, in the IRA stronghold of Andersonstown. On the way, Niedermayer spotted a passing army patrol and tried to attract their attention, but he was brutally pistol-whipped about the head by his kidnappers. When they reached the safe house, Niedermayer, hurt, dazed and confused, was bundled into a small bedroom.

Grundig received a phone call saying that Niedermayer was alive and well. It's probable that the kidnappers attempted to open up some channel of communication with the British government through the intelligence services. But Niedermayer didn't live long enough to be of use to his captors. He died within days of being taken, though the facts of what happened didn't emerge until seven years later, after workmen found his body in a shallow grave at Colin Glen, a local beauty spot on the outskirts of Andersonstown. In 1981, John Bradley, a former IRA training officer, admitted he was one of those assigned to guard the prisoner, who he was told was taken as insurance against the lives of the two sisters. He said that, early in the evening of the third day of the kidnapping, there was a scuffle.

Niedermayer had tried to escape, making a break for the stairs, and he was being held down on the landing. Bradley said: 'We tried to calm him down but he would not stay quiet, he kept yelling. Someone suggested we should gag him or try to knock him out. His nerves were going and he was raving. We tied his hands behind his back and tied his legs, but he was still trying to scream and struggle. We more or less tied him for his own safety. One of the other men hit him with the butt of an automatic pistol to try to knock him out, but he did not stop screaming. We held his face down on the mattress. I think I had his back and legs. We held him for I don't know how long. He was still struggling, but then he went limp and somebody said the man was dead.' The following night, he and two other IRA men took the body to Colin Glen and buried it. 'We put his body face down and we said a prayer over it, then we filled in the grave and said another prayer. I felt drained after what I had been through – the whole episode was not very pleasant. We had no intention of harming him at any time. We had been told to get him everything he wanted and to be as helpful as possible.' Bradley, who admitted the manslaughter of Niedermayer, was jailed for twenty years.

The death of a middle-aged family man, successful businessman, popular employer and innocent bystander in the Troubles was a disaster for the IRA from a propaganda point of view. But at least some Volunteers were willing to try another kidnapping. Internment had led not only to a major upsurge in violence in the North but also created a leadership vacuum within the movement that allowed a number of rogue units to carry out operations without sanction from above.

In the early summer of 1974, Marian and Dolours Price were reported to be close to death. At the beginning of June, doctors reckoned they had little more than a week to live. They had refused food for 205 days, and force-feeding was stopped after one of the sisters lost consciousness during the process. Dolours, 23, and Marian, 20, both student teachers, were daughters of Albert Price, the well known republican from West Belfast and were members of an IRA unit that had brought terror to the streets of London. The Provisionals, like the Fenians a century before them, had decided to take their war directly to England. The date for the start of the bombing campaign, 8 March 1973, was chosen to coincide with a vote in the North on whether or not the border should be retained. That morning, two car bombs, which had been brought over on the Dublin to Liverpool ferry and then driven to London, exploded outside the Old Bailey and the Ministry of Agriculture building in Whitehall. Two other devices – one outside Scotland Yard and one in the West End – were defused before they could go off , but one man died and 250 were injured in the operation. The getaway plan was a disaster. The entire active service unit was picked up at Heathrow Airport as they fled back to Ireland on consecutively numbered tickets. Marian and Dolours Price were among eight people jailed for life for their roles in the bombings.

The two sisters and two other members of the bomb team, Hugh Feeney and Gerard Kelly, requested that they be transferred back to Northern Ireland, where, under a special regime, they would enjoy *de facto* prisoner of war status. The sisters would have been sent to Armagh prison, while

Feeney and Kelly would have ended up in Long Kesh, a Second World War-style prison where prisoners were held in Nissen huts inside a barbed wire compound, were exempted from prison work and operated under a military command. But their request was turned down. All four embarked on a hunger strike and were joined by Francis Stagg and Michael Gaughan, two Republican prisoners in Parkhurst on the Isle of Wight, who wanted to secure political status within the British prison system.

When the Conservatives were ousted from power in 1974, the problem of the hunger-strikers passed to Harold Wilson's Labour government. At first, they appeared split on how to handle it. The Northern Ireland secretary of State, Merlyn Rees, was against concessions. In his memoirs he recalled: 'What the Provisionals wanted was their London-based team back home where its members could bask in political status.' But what he really feared was an IRA attempt to spring the two sisters, who were trophy prisoners, from Armagh women's prison, where he felt security needed to be tightened. Home secretary Roy Jenkins took a softer line, agreeing that it was 'possible and reasonable' for all six prisoners to serve the bulk of their sentences in the North. But Jenkins couldn't be seen to be bullied into it. There were, he said, thirty other Irish prisoners in British jails for terrorist offences. 'Am I to transfer them all under the pressure of the hunger strikes of some?' he asked, 'Or am I to differentiate between those to whom most attention has been drawn, while treating less favourably those who have remained obscure by obeying the law?'

While signalling no change in the Government's position,

his tone was at least more conciliatory than Edward Heath's government's had been. It didn't assuage any of the prisoners. Marian and Dolours Price said they would carry their hunger fast through to its conclusion and the campaign for their demands to be met grew in strength as the sisters wilted. Bishop Edward Daly of Derry and a number of backbench Labour MPs called on Jenkins to back down on humanitarian grounds. Fianna Fáil leader Jack Lynch accused the British government of hypocrisy. Their supposed determination not to give in to intimidation, he said, didn't extend to the militant unionists who had been allowed to topple the North's power-sharing executive that same week.

On Sunday, 2 June, 1974 Albert Price visited his daughters at a special observation unit at Brixton prison and later told reporters waiting outside: 'My daughters will now die. There is no chance they will call off their action on the basis of long-term promises.'

❖❖❖

While it was the image of two young sisters prepared to go right to the end with their death fast that grabbed headlines across the world, it was the two prisoners in Parkhurst – Gaughan and Stagg – who were deteriorating quickest. Both men were critically ill. Stagg had been six months into a ten-year sentence for conspiracy when he first refused food. He began his imprisonment at Albany on the Isle of Wight, where he refused to do prison work and demanded prisoner of war status. He was sent to the punishment block. He was joined by Paul Holms, another of the London car bombers, and Gaughan, who was serving seven years for a bank robbery in North London that netted just £530 for the Official IRA.

The conditions to which they were subjected during their three months in the punishment block persuaded all three to start refusing food. Stagg claimed that they were kept in cells no more than eight feet square, where they had to wash, eat, sleep and use the toilet, while rats came in through the windows at night. On 10 April 1974, eleven days after the start of their fast, the three were shifted to the hospital wing of Parkhurst. Holms ended his strike after he was allowed to wear his own clothes, but Stagg and Gaughan continued to refuse food and, like the Prices, were forcibly fed. Gaughan's throat was badly cut and several of his teeth loosened during the procedure.

On 2 June 1974, Gaughan, in his enfeebled state, contracted pneumonia. The following day, Monday, 3 June, he died, aged twenty-four.The eldest in a family of six children from Ballina, County Mayo now acquired martyr status, as the first Irish prisoner to die on hunger strike in an English jail since Terence McSwiney, the Lord Mayor of Cork, starved himself in Brixton in 1920. Stagg was certain to die next, and Marian and Dolours Price after him.

❖❖❖

On the day after Gaughan's death, a rogue IRA border unit was driving around the Irish countryside, looking for someone to kidnap, in an angry, confused gesture of retaliation. Joe Phelan noticed them taking a great interest in Knocklofty House around 2pm that day, 4 June, but as the day wore on he became preoccupied with other things and thought no more about it.

Just before eleven o'clock that night, there was a knock on the door of the Phelan home in the gate lodge of Knocklofty House. Joe and his friend, Don McGrath, a local farmer, were watching television in the livingroom with Joe's parents, Tom and Bridget. Tom answered the door to find three men standing outside, all of them brandishing revolvers. Two had nylon stockings over their faces. The third man was unmasked, but Tom barely had time to look at his face before he was shoved backwards into the hall and hit across the face with the butt of a gun, while the two masked men charged into the living room and ordered Bridget, Joe and Donal to lie face down on the floor. From a sack they produced more stockings, which were used to tie the four up. Their hands and feet were pushed towards the small of their backs and bound. Bridget suffered from arthritis and had difficulty joining her hands together behind her, so one of the gang members 'assisted' by putting his foot between her shoulder blades. The other masked man ran upstairs to the bedroom where Tom and Bridget's seventeen-year-old daughter, Patricia, was sleeping. Shaken awake by a man wearing a stocking mask, she was told to 'Get up and shut up' before being shoved down the stairs at gunpoint and into the living room, where she was tied up alongside her parents and the others.

The unmasked man did all the talking. It was a hold-up, he said. They were interested in whatever guns were kept at Knocklofty and wanted to know the easiest way into the main house fifty yards up the driveway. Tom told him, truthfully, to go to the front door and ring the bell and was cracked across the back of the head with a gun and kicked in the face. Patricia looked up to see if her father was hurt and was kicked a number of times in the ribs. Fearing they were about to die, Bridget told the family to say an Act of Contrition with her, and she too was hit across the back of the head with a gun.

After several minutes of repeated questions about guns and the layout of the Donoughmore house, the gang decided to go along with Tom's original suggestion and the two masked men were dispatched to the house to try the front door. Despite what the gang had said, robbery wasn't the motive for the raid. While guns would have been a nice bonus, they had actually come for Lord and Lady Donoughmore, to hold them as collateral against the lives of the hunger strikers.

❖❖❖

Lord Donoughmore was born John Michael Henry Hely-Hutchinson in 1902 and was the seventh Earl of Donoughmore. Although English by birth, he spent most of his adult life in Ireland, on the estate in south Tipperary that the family had owned since 1771. His background was the classic upper class archetype. He was educated at Oxford, served in the army during the Second World War and was the Conservative MP for Peterborough between October 1943 and June 1945. Two years after losing his parliamentary seat, he and his wife Jeannie – Dorothy Jean Hetham, MBE – moved to Ireland. They were an outgoing, popular couple. Lady Donoughmore was president of the Clonmel

Flower Show and an active member of the Irish Country-woman's Association, while her husband was a pillar of the horseracing community. He was a steward for the Irish Turf Club, a keen steeplechase rider and owned a string of successful racehorses. As befitted his background, he was also Grandmaster of the Freemason Order in Ireland and a former master of the South Tipperary hunt.

According to Mark Hely-Hutchinson, their son, who later became chief executive of the Bank of Ireland:

I think the mistake the gang made was in thinking my parents were somehow connected to the Royal Family. My mother and father really had no English connection at all, so taking them hostage wasn't a very clever thing to do. They weren't members of the British establishment by any means. My father had for about a year been a Conservative MP, but he was never really a political figure. Politics had never been his life.

He was actually in the army during the Second World War, in the tank regiment. Then he got involved in a staff job in scientific development. The main development he was involved in was a project called FIDO. It stood for Fog Intense, Disposal Of. It always makes me laugh the way the army bends words to come up with acronyms. The project involved getting rid of fog off airport runways. They had these huge burners, which they lined up along the sides of the runway to create enough heat to disperse the fog. I'm not sure if it was really particularly successful, but anyway this was the project he spent a lot of the war working on.

Then, before the end of the war, he became a Conservative MP. I don't think he was ever a Conservative by conviction. He was a Conservative because tradition said that people from the background he came from would be on the Tory side rather than on the Labour side. Anyway, he got in after a by-election. He was still in uniform when he fought it. But then there was a General Election shortly afterwards, in which there was a big swing to Labour and most Conservatives lost their seats. He'd always been planning to live in Ireland and he decided at the conclusion of the war, having been thrown out of Parliament, that this was the moment to return home to Ireland.

It seems unlikely that the kidnappers believed the British government would place any special value on the lives of the Donoughmores. The couple were not, in fact, their original target. They were a Plan B or possibly even a Plan C, after their original abduction plan failed. The chosen target had been the Marquis of Waterford who, unlike the Donoughmores, *was* related to the Royal Family. But when the gang arrived at Curraghmore House, his spectacular castle home in Portlaw just outside Waterford, they found that the Marquis was not at home. It was the week of the Derby and he was at Epsom.

This lack of basic intelligence on the target was symptomatic of a kidnapping plot that was more than just ad hoc; it was farcical. 'It was a complete fiasco,' according to one IRA man from the time.

> You had this unit driving around the Irish countryside with this fucking book, a hardback, *The Stately Homes of Ireland*, and they had it spread out on their laps. This is what they were working from. Pictures of rich people's homes. They decided first of all to go to Waterford to kidnap someone who was related somehow to the Royal Family. No planning, nothing. He was in England at the

races. They abort the mission. They flick through the book again and they find another big house somewhere in Wicklow. They were going to take Sir Alfred Beit. No luck there either. Abort again. So they go back to the book and they find Knocklofty House in Tipperary, which was where the Earl of Donoughmore lived.

The Donoughmores weren't at home either. They were twelve miles away in Fethard, having dinner with Conor Carrigan, an old friend of the peer from his time at Oxford, and his wife, Ines.

Meanwhile, the two masked men went to the front of Knocklofty house and tried the bell, but failed to raise anyone. The butler, his assistant, the cook and the housemaid were all inside, sleeping. So was the nanny, who was looking after two of the Donoughmore grandchildren, James, 7, and Anne, 5, while their parents, Mark Hely-Hutchinson, then assistant managing director of Guinness, and his wife Margaret were enjoying a cruise on the Shannon. Not realising that the front door was unlocked, the two raiders returned to the gate house, where the Phelan family's ordeal continued.

There were more questions and more violence. Tom was kicked and hit again with a gun. Patricia, who was lying on the floor, had the living-room door repeatedly slammed against her head. Then the gang said they were going to take her out and get her to show them a way into the house. Fearing for his sister, Joe offered to take them around to an entrance at the back of the house. The unmasked man and one of the others freed Joe's legs. First, they marched him up to the front of the house, where they pushed the front door, but it didn't move. It was a temperamental one that required a slight kick as the handle was turned, but Joe didn't tell them that. He led them around the back of the house and indicated a door, which turned out to be locked.

As the Donoughmores returned from their night out, they noticed an unfamiliar car parked outside the gatehouse, but the Phelans often had guests so they thought nothing of it. Inside, the man holding the family at gunpoint heard the Renault 4 go by and chased after it, having warned the Phelan family that he would kill them if they cooperated with the Gardaí.

At the back of Knocklofty House, Joe and the two raiders heard the sound of the car crunching its way up the gravel driveway. The unmasked man, who was clearly the leader, ordered Joe to sit on the ground, while the other raced around to the front of the house. There was a loud bang that sounded like a gunshot. It was probably nothing more than a warning shot fired by the gang member leaving the gatehouse in order to alert the others to the couple's arrival, but the leader feared it was a Garda ambush and ran around to the front of the house too.

Lord and Lady Donoughmore were both in formal evening dress when they got out of their car. Lord Donoughmore planned to let his three pet Labradors out for a run, but before he reached the door he heard his wife shout: 'Who are you?'

In a personal account of the kidnapping that he wrote in the days after his release, Lord Donoughmore recalled:

I saw a man carrying a long-barrelled revolver, wearing two

stockings in the form of a mask, running towards me. He ran past me, between me and the house, and I saw three other small types (a fourth man had appeared) waving guns, telling us to lie down.

Lord Donoughmore's handwritten diary, which has been seen by the author, offers a fascinating insight into the abduction. Intended for his family, it is written in the 'stiff upper lip' tradition that was part and parcel of his upbringing and is punctuated by moments of high farce that, consciously or otherwise, play down the danger they faced. In fact, it reads like some breathless, Blytonish adventure.

He wrote that on the return journey from Fethard that night – on the road between Clonmel and home – Lady Donoughmore told her husband she thought a car was following them. Three-quarters of a mile from Knocklofty the car turned off. Whether this was just a coincidence or a member of the gang had actually been sent to check up on them is never made clear.

Back at the house, the couple put up a fight and there was a violent struggle. Lord Donoughmore was hit three times across the head with the butt of a gun and recalled that the strap of his watch was broken as he held his hands up to protect his head. His wife, he wrote, gave a far better account of herself, biting the leader on the hand and landing 'a good left hook,' which damaged her forefinger. When they were subdued, they were dragged across the gravel and into the stolen Cortina, which tore off down the driveway with the couple wedged between two gang members in the back. Outside the entrance to the estate the car stopped for a moment and thick adhesive tape was used to cover the couple's eyes. They then took off again in the direction of Dublin.

They drove for what Lord Donoughmore estimated was about two hours, 'a nightmare drive' along winding, badly pocked roads. The most violent member of the gang, whom he christened 'Terror Man', had a map in front of him and barked directions at the driver. Lady Donoughmore was sick in the back of the car and 'Terror Man' threatened to have her gagged when she started fretting about James and Anne, their two grandchildren back at Knocklofty.

The car stopped in Blessington, County Wicklow. The couple were ordered out and made to sit on marshy ground for ten minutes, while they waited for another car to arrive. Lady Donoughmore had been cracked across the head with a gun during the struggle and she was in pain.

'If you hadn't resisted, you wouldn't have been hurt,' the gang leader told her. She replied: 'Would *you* have resisted?' at which point he laughed and said, 'I suppose I would.'

The second car arrived and the Cortina was abandoned and set alight. They drove for a short time and changed cars again to further disorientate the couple.

They stopped at a remote bungalow, close to the border between Laois and Kildare, which was owned by a republican sympathiser who'd agreed to make himself scarce for a week. The Donoughmores were taken into a small, fourteen-foot square room that contained two hard chairs and a sofa bed, which they sat on during the day and slept on at night, while four masked men worked tandem shifts keeping them under armed guard. Once inside the room, a safety razor was used to hack off their makeshift blindfolds.

When Lord Donoughmore's eyes adjusted to the light in the room, he saw two men, wearing black hoods, standing over him. He wrote: 'I couldn't help but say, "My God, you look like the Ku Klux Klan."' The leader told them not to try to escape or they'd be shot. Lord Donoughmore said, rather innocently, that they couldn't escape because his wife had no shoes. She'd lost one in the struggle back at Knocklofty and one in the Cortina.

The curtains were kept closed and the light left permanently on. At night a box was placed over the bulb to dim the room enough to allow the captives to sleep. According to Lord Donoughmore's account, he and his wife slept surprisingly well that night. The sound of cattle being brought off for their early morning milking announced the beginning of their first day as unwitting actors in a deadly drama, as Harold Wilson's government and the IRA played brinkmanship together.

❖❖❖

The kidnap gang weren't the only ones trying to force a quick end to the stalemate that the hunger strikers and the British government had talked themselves into. Paddy Devlin, a founder member of the SDLP and a one-time IRA Volunteer himself, phoned Home Secretary Roy Jenkins and offered to act as a broker, to try to find a way in which both sides could get out without losing face. The loyalist-engineered collapse of power sharing had already destroyed the nationalist community's faith in constitutional politics. Only the IRA could benefit from the death of the hunger strikers. Making martyrs of the Price sisters, he warned, would lead to a swing back to the politics of the gun, as would happen when ten hunger strikers died in the North seven years later. The Provisionals issued a statement that weekend, saying: 'The IRA make no threat. We simply state that, as comrades of these girls, we shall not rest until just retribution is exacted from Mr Wilson and his servants. No British government shall murder citizens of Ireland and expect to get away scot-free.'

Devlin saw a sliver of light in Jenkins's statement that it would be 'reasonable and possible' for all the hunger strikers to serve the bulk of their sentences in Northern Ireland. He put forward a compromise whereby the prisoners would agree to call off their fast in return for a secret agreement to return them to the North within an agreed timeframe. But Jenkins was still reluctant to commit himself to a date, while the IRA wanted to know what would happen if there was a change of Government in the interim. As it happened, they had far more to fear from Labour than from the Conservatives. The 1974 stand-off was a precursor to the eventual decision by Merlyn Rees to withdraw effective prisoner of war status from all those jailed during the Troubles, thereby criminalising what had previously been treated as political crimes.

On Tuesday, 4 June, Devlin visited the Price sisters in the hospital wing of Brixton prison and persuaded them that Jenkins was prepared to meet them on some middle ground. He promised to return the following morning with two witnesses to any agreement that was made. That night he phoned Jenkins, who suggested Lord Brockway, an elderly Labour peer who, he said, had considerable knowledge of Irish affairs, and Jock Stallard, the Labour MP for St

Pancras North who was a member of the party's Northern Ireland Committee. Devlin went to bed that night convinced that a huge step towards saving the lives of the sisters and the other three surviving hunger strikers had been taken.

❖❖❖

The Donoughmores' son, Mark, was asleep in his boat on the Shannon when a Garda arrived around dawn on 5 June to tell him his parents had been kidnapped. 'This poor, unfortunate Garda had to walk this long length of the Shannon, knocking on the door of cruisers, asking, "Are you Mark Hely-Hutchinson?"' he recalls.

> They actually found us very quickly. The Shannon is very well organised in that at every lock they keep a log of who's been through. So by ringing up lock keepers they could tell which two- or three-mile stretch of the river we were on. When he mentioned something about a kidnapping we all went into shock. He said we needed to get back to Knocklofty as quickly as possible, presumably in case the kidnappers wanted to make contact, because we presumed at that stage that it was a straight case of a ransom demand. We were never told anything about the Price sisters or anything like that until it was all over. We assumed throughout it was going to be a matter of paying over money to get my parents back.
>
> In fact, the Gardaí advised us to have some money ready just in case there was a demand. So we organised it. We raided my father's account in the bank in Clonmel. We talked to the manager and we said, 'Listen, this is his money and this is him who's being held for ransom. Surely it's reasonable to ask for it.' And the manager

agreed. My father was very upset about that afterwards. 'How dare the bank give them my money?'

It might have been about twenty thousand pounds, maybe fifty thousand, something like that. We were given it in used notes and we literally made a manual record of the serial numbers on all the notes. There were several family members there in the house and we spent a day-and-a-half or something going through those damn notes, recording all of the numbers on paper, so the police might trace the money later. We waited and waited for the call, but it never came.

No ransom demand was ever made, leading Gardaí to believe that the gang was talking to somebody else, probably British intelligence. They did, in fact, open a channel of communication that would be used to help bring about the Peace Process twenty years later. According to one IRA source:

They made a contact that proved very useful later on in bringing about the 1994 ceasefire. We're not talking about MI5 or MI6. They weren't spooks with guns. It was a quasi-political contact. The phone calls were made from Belfast. There wasn't any real dialogue involved. It was a simple case of, 'We've got this couple and we're gonna fucking shoot them.' It had no bearing at all on the decision to send the Price sisters home, but the channel stayed open. We used it from time to time, if we wanted something to be known. And when it was time for the ceasefire it came in very handy.

In contrast to the violent assault they suffered back at Knocklofty, Lord and Lady Donoughmore were treated well once they were ensconced inside the safe house. Only two members of the original snatch team remained with them – the men they came to know as 'the leader' and 'the lieutenant'. Two locals were also brought in to watch over them, but were ordered not to talk for fear that their accents would pinpoint the location of the house.

All four seem to have been unfailingly courteous to the couple. The elderly peer and his wife, members of the landed gentry, sharing the same cramped space with two young, hardened republican gunmen, produced what, from Lord Donoughmore's account, was a surreal and slightly comic atmosphere in the house. Breakfast on the first day, he records, consisted of bread and butter and an egg that was overboiled almost to the point of being inedible. Lunch was meat, peas and mashed potato, but the gang leader sur-passed himself by cooking a traditional Irish fry for dinner, including sausages, bacon and, he writes enthusiastically, one of the nicest, softest fried eggs he'd ever tasted. His wife told the lieutenant to pass on their compliments to the chef and he returned later to say the chef was grateful: 'He wants to know if there'd be a job at Knocklofty for him when this is all over.'

Mark Hely-Hutchinson says that his father decided to commit his account of what happened to paper as an act of catharsis. It's quite possible that in dramatising this episode he was suppressing those moments when, inevitably, the couple were confused or frightened for their lives. But they do seem to have forged a genuine relationship with their captors, with jokes flying back and forth between them. Lord Donoughmore believed the leader was very charmed by his wife, especially by her courage. 'My father said that one of the kidnappers was beginning to fall in love with Jeannie, my mother, because he'd probably never met anybody quite like her before.'

It is quite probable that the Donoughmores were showing signs of the psychological phenomenon that had recently been defined as Stockholm Syndrome. Psychologists believe that abused people often try to form a bond with their abuser as a means of enduring their ordeal. In hostage situations this means that victims often display an association or empathy with their captors. The phenomenon was discovered in 1973 after a prison escapee, Jan-Erik Olsson, held four bank staff at gunpoint in a vault for six days after a botched robbery attempt on the Sveriges Kreditbank in Stockholm. Interviewed afterwards, the four staff showed an unusual affinity with their captor and a strange hostility towards the police who ended their ordeal. Long-term studies of hundreds of similar hostage situations have defined a clear and characteristic set of symptoms that correspond closely to Lord Donoughmore's account of his and his wife's feelings during their kidnapping.

Soon after they were taken hostage, the couple began trying to form an impression in their minds of the kidnappers. The leader, they reckoned, was from Belfast and was as young as twenty-six or twenty-seven. He may have had a medical background. On their first night at the house he brought them a basin of water and some Dettol to bathe the wounds they had received in the struggle at Knocklofty. Something in the way he did it led Lord Donoughmore to ask whether he had medical training. He replied, 'No, only first aid,' but Donoughmore didn't believe him. From his accent, they thought that the lieutenant hailed from one of the Ulster counties in the Republic.

The leader was, in fact, a well-known IRA man from the Falls Road who later served as Belfast commander. He was a friend and ally of Gerry Adams and was one of the organisation's most charasmatic figures. The lieutenant, as Lord Donoughmore described him, was Eddie Gallagher, an IRA renegade from Ballybofey, County Donegal, who would meet his Waterloo after another kidnapping in a house just a few miles from where the Donoughmores were held.

❖❖❖

Gallagher was a drifter and dreamer who was described by the prosecuting counsel who helped put him away as living 'on the lunatic edge of revolutionary mania'. The unit in which he operated was the IRA's most flamboyant and daring, but the leadership barely tolerated him. He was rash and unpredictable, but he was also prolific, and a number of spectacular operations, including the theft of the Beit paintings and an attempt to bomb an RUC station in Strabane in a hijacked helicopter, had won him and his unit many admirers, especially among the old romantics who fought the Border Campaign of the late 1950s and early 1960s.

The unit was self-financed and effectively fighting its own war. While working in construction in England, Gallagher had met and fallen in love with Rose Dugdale, the daughter of a wealthy Lloyds underwriter, Lieutenant Colonel James Dugdale. She was the heiress to his fortune. Her money gave the gang the freedom to operate independently of the IRA's command structure, while an extensive network of contacts and safe houses allowed them to pop up anywhere and at any time and to disappear again just as quickly.

Dugdale was drawn towards anarchist politics while studying at Oxford and later at London University, where she earned a PhD. She revolted against her upper class background, teaming up with a gang of professional thieves to steal £80,000 worth of silver, jewellery and antiques from her father's home in Axminster, Devon. In October 1973 she received a two-year suspended prison sentence for her part in the robbery. But it was television pictures of British paratroopers shooting dead unarmed civil right protesters in Derry in 1972 that really fired Dugdale's revolutionary zeal. She began operating with Gallagher and other members of the unit in Britain and was behind various plots to smuggle arms and explosives into the North. In 1973 she persuaded a number of English criminal friends to pose as campers while they toured north Wales looking for explosives to steal. In May of that year, an English court later heard, she borrowed a car from a friend, cut the springs out of the back seat and hid a parcel in it containing a stengun, a .38 revolver, an automatic pistol and ammunition, which she said were 'for the boys'. She persuaded a friend to take the car across to Northern Ireland on the Stranraer to Larne ferry.

In February 1974 Manchester police issued a warrant for Dugdale's arrest in relation to a conspiracy to smuggle arms. But by then she had already fled to Ireland with Gallagher. The two began operating around the border area, but within months she was caught in possession of the stolen Beit paintings and at the time of the Donoughmore kidnapping was in prison awaiting trial. She was also pregnant with Gallagher's child and it was her jailing that eventually sent him off the rails. 'Eddie was like a big child,' says one IRA Volunteer who knew him.

> He was very brave. Very intelligent. Very charming. A very likable guy. But he was immature. I mean, he was like a schoolkid. He'd say, 'Let's grab a fucking minister.' You'd have to ask him, 'Well, okay, but to what end?' and he wouldn't have thought it through. He was unpredictable like that. He was agitated, on edge the whole time. Just very immature. He couldn't be told anything, which was part of the reason it was decided to do something about him at the end. To be honest, I always saw him as more of a revolutionary than a republican. He had no background in the Troubles. But he was always sloganising. He was full of socialist rhetoric. It was revolution he was more interested in.

Gallagher didn't come from a classic republican background. He was born in Ballybofey, the son of a dairy farmer who voted for Fianna Fáil but otherwise had no strong political leanings. His mother died when he was twelve, which may have contributed to him being quiet and sensitive as a boy. Despite the sharp political awareness he developed in his late teens, he wasn't much of a student and left the local technical school without sitting any exams. He went to England to work as a labourer with his older brother, Paddy, who was a subcontractor in the midlands. During slack periods he would return to Donegal where he worked in a petrol station and did casual work on neighbours' farms. Gallagher became politicised during his years in England and was fascinated by left-wing revolutionaries.

He first came to the attention of the authorities in the summer of 1973. He was arrested along with Thomas Dignam and Joe Coughlan, two IRA men from County Offaly, after they were spotted acting suspiciously in Donegal town. One of the three had a list of materials on him which included an alarm clock, bell wire, batteries, plastic tape, clothes pegs and micro-switches, while a bottle discovered in the back of the car contained a substance that later turned out to be gunpowder. After they were brought in for questioning, Coughlan took the desk sergeant to one side and told him to ring the Garda station at Pettigo – a small pinprick of a village that straddles the border between Donegal and Fermanagh – to tell them to have the streets cleared. Some time afterwards a car bomb exploded on the Fermanagh side of the border but caused minimal damage. In a statement, Gallagher claimed that the bottle of gunpowder was left in his car by another man who had not told him what it contained. The three, who refused to recognise the court, were each given four-month sentences for causing malicious damage, but were cleared of the more serious charge of possessing explosives.

Gallagher was out again within a matter of weeks, having had plenty of time to plot his next move. He was forever scheming – gathering intelligence on banks and post offices, and details of transfers of large amounts of money, with a view to possible robberies, as well as keeping an eye on the movements of significant people as potential kidnap victims. His attention span was short and he had a dozen or more of these plans jostling for position in his mind at any one time. He operated with a unit around the border area but travelled back and forth to England, where he carried out operations. But what he really longed for was the big spectacular job that would make his name. Dugdale's forte was commercial sabotage and the two came up with a tentative plan to try to put Lloyds out of business by blowing up their computers.

Because of her background and connections, Dugdale was regarded with suspicion by the IRA leadership. Some believed she was a British agent. Others doubted she had any genuine empathy with the nationalist struggle, seeing her as a confused young woman, rebelling, like Patty Hearst, against her upper-class upbringing. But among the grassroots she won a grudging respect for her courage and daring.

❖❖❖

On 23 January 1974, Gallagher and Dugdale travelled to the village of Gortahork on the west coast of Donegal and checked into McFadden's Hotel as man and wife to plan an assault on the joint RUC and British Army base across the border in Strabane, County Tyrone. Dugdale posed as a journalist to persuade John Hobday, a thirty-five-year-old helicopter pilot, to fly her to Tory Island to take some aerial photographs. She chartered the small Bolkow 105D, using the name Stephanie Grant and giving an address in Leeds. Hobday met her in McFadden's that night, when she was in the company of Gallagher and two other men, who he was told were also journalists who were interested in seeing the island. They set off the following morning, but three miles out over the Atlantic, near the island of Inishbofin, a gun was produced and Hobday was ordered to return to Ards Pier in Gortahork, where four milk churns, each packed with over a hundred pounds of explosives, were loaded on board. Two eventually had to be ditched because they were weighing the helicopter down. The pilot was ordered to fly the forty miles to Strabane, where they twice passed low over the barracks. On the third pass, the churns were pushed out. Both missed their target and failed to explode. Hobday was instructed to fly back across the border to Cloughfinn, where the gang hijacked a car to make their escape.

In February the same gang was almost certainly behind the theft of a million-pound painting in England, the event that appears to have first signalled Dugdale's identification with the suffering of Marian and Dolours Price. *The Guitar Player*, one of Vermeer's late masterpieces, was stolen from Kenwood House gallery in London. In a letter to the *Times* newspaper, the thieves demanded that the two sisters, as well as Hugh Feeney and Gerry Kelly, be returned to Northern Ireland to serve their sentences, and enclosed a strip cut from the canvas to show that it wasn't a hoax. A second letter warned that the painting would be burned on St Patrick's Day unless the demand was met. After a tip-off, the painting was found ten weeks later in St Bartholomew's churchyard in London, propped up against a headstone and wrapped in a copy of the *London Evening News*. By that time the gang had pulled off an even more spectacular art theft, one that would cost Dugdale her freedom and send Gallagher on the desperate spiral that led to his own capture the following year.

On the night of Friday 26 April, 1974 Rose Dugdale rang the doorbell of Russborough House, Sir Alfred Beit's secluded mansion just outside Blessington, County Wicklow. A member of staff opened the door after he heard her say something in French. Four men rushed out of the darkness at him, knocked him to the floor and held a gun to his neck. The *modus operandi* was almost identical to the raid on Knocklofty six weeks later. The gang arrived in a stolen Ford Cortina. Sir Alfred Beit was struck across the head with a revolver before he, his wife and the house staff were corralled into the library and, like the Phelan family, tied up using nylon stockings that the gang had brought with them. They then used a screwdriver to cut nineteen paintings, including a Vermeer, a Goya, two Gainsboroughs and three Rubens, from their frames.

From the beginning, the Gardaí knew that the Russborough raid was more than a simple art theft. The paintings were so unique as to be impossible to sell on. Only one Vermeer painting, for instance, had changed hands on the open market since 1932. The gang issued their demands a few days later in a letter to James White, the director of the National Gallery in Dublin. Five of the paintings would be returned as soon as the four hunger strikers were moved to Northern Ireland. The other fourteen would be returned on payment of a £500,000 ransom. The letter warned that unless both demands were fulfilled by 14 May, the art collection, which was valued at £8m, would be burned .The Gardaí may have got some clue as to who they were looking for from the verbal abuse hurled at the paintings' owners during the robbery. Sir Alfred, a multi-millionaire financier

and member of a wealthy South African diamond fan was called a 'capitalist pig' and accused of exploiting wo ers. The Gardaí eventually caught up with Dugdale and th stolen paintings at a cottage in Glandore, County Cork, which she had rented as a safe house for Gallagher and the unit. In June 1974 she was jailed for nine years.

❖❖❖

While the Gardaí were never contacted by the Knocklofty kidnappers, they were convinced from the outset that it was Gallagher's gang that had Lord and Lady Donoughmore. The operation bore all the hallmarks of the Russborough robbery, for which Gallagher was still being sought for questioning.

The search was concentrated in a triangle of countryside between Tipperary, Cork and Waterford, with thousands of soldiers and Gardaí with sniffer dogs combing vast tracts of land around Clogheen, Ballyporeen and Araglen, where Gallagher was a familiar face. They searched vacant buildings and sheds around the Knockmealdown and Galty Mountains, but were miles away from where the couple were actually being held.

On Wednesday morning, 5 June, at the start of the Donoughmores' first full day in captivity, Gallagher and the leader sat down with the couple and wrote out a list of everything they needed, including toothbrushes, soap and fresh clothes, as their old ones were covered in blood from the fight the night before. They were asked for their sizes in trousers and shoes. Lord Donoughmore was down in the dumps because he was going to miss the Epsom Derby that

afternoon. He asked the leader whether he could find out the result for him but he seemed preoccupied, apparently worried that the house was about to be raided. He came into the room at one point, still wearing his balaclava, put his finger to his lips and then spent a few minutes peering out through a tiny crack in the curtains. After a while he relaxed again. At this stage, the couple still presumed they were being held for a cash ransom.

The fresh clothes arrived that night and so did the first bit of news from the outside world. The leader told them that their eldest son, Lord Suirdale, who ran a financial consultancy in Paris, had just been on the radio, offering a substantial ransom for their safe return. Lady Donoughmore wondered aloud what the family valued them at and said she hoped it was low, as it was they, in the end, who would have to pay it. The leader laughed at that. Lady Donoughmore said, 'I suppose you have us here for money?' The leader said no and told them for the first time that they'd been taken as a kind of insurance policy against the lives of two women who were on hunger strike in an English prison and who might die at any minute. Lord Donoughmore dared not ask what would happen to him and his wife if they did. It's the only point in his account at which he admits to being frightened and also angry. He wrote: 'He thought the kidnapping of a lord would influence Mr Wilson. I said nonsense, and I said that if I was bumped off for such a silly reason I'd be very annoyed.'

❖❖❖

The couple weren't aware of it, but Wednesday had been a

good day for them. In London it looked as though the hunger strike was drawing to a happy conclusion. That afternoon, Roy Jenkins agreed in principle to the idea of returning the five surviving prisoners to the North within a set timeframe – probably a year – so as not to look as though he'd been coerced into it. On Thursday morning, 6 June, Paddy Devlin went to Brixton with Stallard and Lord Brockway to put what Jenkins had said to the sisters. They agreed to call off their fast, but attached four preconditions: that they be allowed to wear their own clothes while awaiting transfer, that they be exempted from prison work, that they be served with food from outside the prison and that they be allowed to write letters to internees at Long Kesh. On Thursday night Devlin again spoke to Jenkins, who agreed to the four preconditions.

The sword hanging over the heads of the elderly peer and his wife does not seem to have exerted any greater urgency on Devlin and Jenkins to find a way to end the hunger strike. The kidnapping doesn't even merit a mention in Devlin's account of the negotiations in his memoirs. As for Jenkins, the thought of two young women martyring themselves in a British prison, on his beat, was enough in itself to concentrate his mind on the issue.

On Thursday morning, one of the gang brought Lord Donoughmore the racing page from that morning's newspaper to let him read about 50-1 shot *Snow Night's* shock win in the Derby. The couple were also given three editions of *Time* magazine from 1973. The day dragged by while the two kidnappers continued to listen to the radio for news on the condition of the Price sisters. They also took several phonecalls from a mysterious third party who seemed to be giving them instructions. Lady Donoughmore tried to kill a couple of hours by doing a crossword puzzle. It produced a moment of hilarity that Lord Donoughmore loved to recall right up until the time of his death. 'Someone had discovered that my mother liked these crossword puzzles,' Mark Hely-Hutchinson says.

> So they brought her one of some sort and she was trying to find the answer to this particular clue – which county wears black and amber colours in the GAA. It was the two local men who were guarding them at the time. And my father just couldn't get the answer. He said, 'it's on the tip of my tongue but I really can't remember who it is'. So they started going through all the letters of the alphabet. They're going through all the As: Antrim. Armagh. They're doing it letter by letter. It's not Donegal. It's not Derry. And eventually, after a few minutes of this, one of these locals, who had been told they must never, ever, speak to my parents, just blurted out, 'Oh for God's sake, it's Kilkenny. Do you not know that?'

At some point a helicopter passed overhead. But the search was futile; the Gardaí simply threw a perfunctory net over all known republican sympathisers to see who they could drag in. They raided homes in all four provinces, including that of Sinn Féin president Ruairí Ó Brádaigh. There were dawn raids in Tipperary, Donegal, Westmeath and Roscommon. In Cahirciveen, County Kerry, Gardaí searched the homes of twelve Official Sinn Féin members and were reported to have seized documents, which turned out to be nothing more incriminating than literature for the upcoming council elections.

❖❖❖

If the gang ever believed that the Irish public would be ambivalent about the fate of a couple of English-born aristocrats, they got a sharp rebuff that Thursday night. Six hundred local people attended a public meeting in Clonmel to demand the safe return of the Donoughmores. Women wept openly at the meeting, while speaker after speaker, from all sorts of backgrounds, stood up to express solidarity with the couple, who were enormously popular in the area.

John Allen, the Mayor of Clonmel, told the meeting: 'There are many images of nationalism and sometimes crimes are committed in its name. But those who know Lord Donoughmore and his lady are only too well aware of their love of our aspirations and our way of life ... We do not know who is responsible for this unfortunate occurrence, and I certainly hesitate to think that there is any local involvement whatsoever. If it is to be taken as an expression of protest by any organisation, north or south of this unnatural border that divides us, then I would urge those concerned to think again in the interests of humanity and to lift the burden of anguish which has fallen across the shoulders of the family of those lovable people. Whoever you are, or whatever your motives, we would appeal to you to restore the happiness of this family and to justify our faith in high ideals by returning this elderly couple, free and safe, to the community which loves, respects and holds them in their hearts.'

And there was a sting in the tail. What the gang wouldn't have read in *The Stately Homes of Ireland* was that Knocklofty House had been a safe haven for IRA men during the War of

Independence. In December 1920, Tipperary, along with Limerick, Cork and Kerry, was placed under martial law, as the British Army, backed by the Black and Tans, pressed to end the uprising which was fiercest in the southern counties. There were hundreds of IRA gunmen on the run in Tipperary and many were billeted at Knocklofty, which probably explains why the house escaped the fate of many other stately homes in the area, which were burnt to the ground.

While Mark Hely-Hutchinson disputes a description of his father from the floor at the Clonmel meeting as being 'more Republican than many within the IRA', he doesn't doubt the house's IRA connection.

> My father never really got involved in politics in this country one way or another, on any side. He always took the view that it wasn't any of his business. I'm not old enough to have been around at the time of the War of Independence, but it was certainly always said that there were various people who were fighting the English who hid out there. That doesn't necessarily mean that the Hely-Hutchinson family were sympathetic to one side or the other, because no one is entirely sure whether they knew what was going on. You have to remember it was a huge estate and there were quite a number of employees who had cottages around the grounds, and we know that some of them had contacts. Certainly, if IRA people did stay in Knocklofty it wasn't because of any connection with the family, but rather with the employees.

On Friday morning, Lord and Lady Donoughmore were awoken by the kidnappers and told about the meeting in Clonmel. Lady Donoughmore reflected that that it was 'the most wonderful thing we heard while we were in captivity' and it bolstered their spirits for what was going to be a long thirty-six hours. The leader told her husband the results of the Coronation Cup, which was run at Epsom the previous day, giving him the first, second and third placings. Lord Donoughmore asked if, as a special treat, he might be allowed listen to the Oaks on the radio on Saturday. The leader said that if things went as well as they expected them to, he would be watching it on television back at Knocklofty.

❖❖❖

The Provisional, IRA were particularly sensitive to political opinion in the Republic at the time and were seething over the kidnapping. Taoiseach Liam Cosgrave, who had met the Donoughmores a few times socially, said that the Government would do everything to track down the unit, and the leadership feared a major crackdown. A source recalls:

> The leadership mightn't have been the strongest at the time, but there was still a command structure within which you had to operate. The units in the North had a lot more freedom. You could do things all over the place without looking for permission. But not in the South. Military operations in the Republic were forbidden by general army orders. And you'd Gallagher and his crowd charging around the place, waving guns, doing robberies, kidnapping people. It was stupid. It was playing into Cosgrave's hands, giving him an excuse to hammer us.

And it wasn't just the Gardaí who were on the trail of the kidnappers. Phil Flynn, the well known republican and trade unionist from Dundalk, took it upon himself to track down the unit and persuade them to release the couple. Flynn, a thirty-four-year-old member of Sinn Féin's *Ard Comhairle* – the Party's decision-making body – and assistant general secretary of the Local Government and Public Services Union, had just been released from Portlaoise Prison, having been acquitted of IRA membership. During one of the routine raids on his home, Special Branch detectives had found a fake cover for a Garda identification tucked inside the pages of an IPA (Institute of Public Administration) diary. Flynn claimed he found it on the ground while out jogging. He didn't know what to do with it, he said, so he put it in his diary, marking the date on which he picked it up. In the end, the fake ID cover wasn't used to support the membership charge and he picked holes in the prosecution case. Someone who was as open about his republican beliefs as he was couldn't be guilty of subversion, he argued, before declaring that he didn't recognise the legitimacy of the court. He was believed to be the first defendant ever to successfully argue his own case before the Special Criminal Court while also using the traditional republican tactic of non-recognition. Flynn, who was close to IRA chief of staff Seamus Twomey, believed the kidnapping was just the excuse Cosgrave wanted to try to crush the Provisionals and that someone had to try to talk sense into Gallagher and his partner. 'Flynn knew Eddie well,' according to a source familiar with the story.

> They went back a few years. He liked him but he was pissed off, the same as a lot of other people, by what he'd done. You just didn't operate like this in the South. This was going to bring all kinds of

trouble down on top of us. Any of the boys who were in Portlaoise in 1973 will tell you what the change of Government did. Before Cosgrave, we had cell searches. You never had them smashing up your cell, smashing up your craftwork, like you did after he got in. And the view was that if the Donoughmores got shot there'd be more legislation against us.

As far as I know, the way it happened was that Flynn started arguing the point with, let's say, mutual acquaintances, saying it was a stupid thing to do, it was playing right into the Government's hands. And then the word came back to Flynn that Gallagher wanted to know what his agenda was. Flynn said his agenda was that if they were stupid enough to carry out a kidnapping in the Republic, then why did they have to target a family with their history of being friendly to republicans? 'Friendly to republicans?' Flynn said yeah, IRA men were put up at Knocklofty during the War of Independence. 'Oh.' They didn't even realise that. But anyway that was how Flynn got word to them that he wanted to talk.

❖ ❖ ❖

In Brixton prison on the morning of Friday, 7 June, the Price sisters were told that Roy Jenkins had agreed to their four preconditions. They told Paddy Devlin that they would end their fast once they had spoken to their parents and to the other hunger strikers. They met their mother and father that afternoon and spoke on the phone with Hugh Feeney in Gartree prison and with Gerry Kelly in Wormwood Scrubs. All of the prisoners agreed to call off their action. At eleven o'clock that night the strike officially ended when a doctor gave the sisters a liquid diet, the first food they had accepted in 213 days.

At around the same time, the light went on in the sitting room where Lord and Lady Donoughmore were sleeping. The leader and Gallagher came in and told them that the hunger strike was over. They'd be released the following night. Lord Donoughmore told them that, for the first time in his life, he was glad that Britain had a Labour government. The Conservatives would never have given in, he suggested. The leader laughed and said, 'Perhaps we wouldn't have taken them on.'

Saturday dragged by, but the atmosphere in the house seems to have been light as the couple and their captors spent what they knew would be their final hours together. The leader brought in a radio and sat in between them on the sofa while they listened to the live commentary on the Oaks. A deck of cards helped them pass a few more hours. The kidnappers taught them how to play Chinese patience.

Night fell and there was still no sign of them being released. The explanation they were given for this was that the Prices still weren't back in Northern Ireland, though this was a ruse. The British hadn't agreed to move them right away. What they were really waiting for was Flynn. Their main concern now was how to extricate themselves from the trouble they were in with the IRA leadership, and they wanted him to use his influence to keep them off their backs. But there was still no sign of him and the couple were told they'd have to spend another night in the house. They begged to stay up for a little while longer, in case there was more news from England. But the sofa bed was pulled out, marking the beginning of an unexpected fifth night in captivity. They dozed off. At some point in the night the door opened and someone said, 'We'll go now'. They hadn't heard the voice before. It was Flynn. According to a Volunteer familiar with the story:

> There wasn't any persuading to be done. He came for the two hostages, and they said, you can take them. He went into the room and told them he was there to release them. They just huddled close together. They thought they were being brought outside to be shot. Flynn just said, 'Come on, before they change their minds'.
>
> They stuck the blindfolds on them – just scarves – and they were brought out to Flynn's car. He drove. The order was that they were to be taken to Dublin, to the Phoenix Park. There were two boys in the car as well; one was from Offaly, the other Kildare. Gallagher would have known them. They took all these back roads, these snaking roads through the countryside, so as to avoid the roadblocks. They'd a car up ahead, scouting the road. And at some point on this S-shaped road it jammed on the brake lights, which was the signal that the guards were up ahead.
>
> So Flynn had to turn the car around and take a different route. But of course now he's lost his scout car. They come into the city down by Islandbridge, and up ahead there's another roadblock. There's a Garda checking cars. Flynn shouts at the others to get the blindfolds off them. The boys put their guns down under the seats. The Garda just waved them through.

Strangely, Lord Donoughmore's diary version of events differs quite significantly from this account. He makes no reference to the mystery figure who arrived in the middle of the night to drive them to freedom. He describes the car that took them to Dublin as being silver, when Flynn's car was in fact red. And he places both the leader and the lieutenant in the vehicle, even though it's unlikely they would have put themselves in the position of being caught with the couple once they'd released them. He even has the leader shaking his hand in the Phoenix Park and bowing to him. There are also inconsistencies between his written account and the story he told a press conference on the day after his release. Then he specifically stated that at no time during the drive to Dublin were their blindfolds removed, but in the written version he says that their eyes were uncovered when they saw a Garda up ahead talking to another motorist. There was no mention of this happening in the story he told the press. In fact, he claimed that they were twice told to lie on the floor as they passed what he guessed were Garda checkpoints. Mark Hely-Hutchinson has always believed that his father changed some aspects of the story out of a confused sense of loyalty to the kidnappers for treating them so well and for releasing them unharmed. He also suspects that he told the Gardaí a lot less than he could have.

> My parents had a very warm relationship with the people who captured them. You can see from what he wrote how it develops over the four days. They were quite fond of them. And I always had a suspicion that my father did know a lot more than he let on. There are references in his account of when they were being let out to the masks no longer being on the kidnappers, and he says he made a point of not looking at them. And this was certainly the story that he told everyone, but I have a suspicion that he actually saw them. I have a suspicion in the back of my mind that my father knew more than he ever let on to anybody. He really, actively, did not want those men to be caught. Because of the relationship.

When the couple were let out of the car, they were ordered to walk in a straight line and not to look back. They did what they were told and arrived at the Parkgate Street entrance to the Phoenix Park. Shortly after 3am they knocked on the door of a nearby house and asked the occupants to call the Gardaí. It was around 5am on Sunday morning when the news reached Knocklofty that they were safe. Meanwhile, Flynn drove the two men towards the city. It was all over. For now anyway.

CHAPTER THREE

Eddie Gallagher's Last Stand
The Taking of Tiede Herrema

*'They said they were soldiers. I said if they were soldiers then I was
entitled to the proper treatment you expect as a
prisoner of war.'* Dr Tiede Herrema

Eddie Gallagher was a man with a mission. On 25 June 1974,
just over two weeks after the Donoughmores were freed,
Rose Dugdale was sentenced to nine years in prison for her
part in the Beit paintings robbery. Further charges were prepared in relation to the Strabane barracks attack. The inde-
fatigable Gallagher began focusing more and more of his
energy on freeing her from Limerick jail, where, he later
claimed, she was seriously ill-treated. None of his various
plans had got beyond the development stage when Gallagher was dramatically arrested in Portlaoise on 15
August. He was drinking in a local pub with Richard Behal,
the well-known republican who famously cut down trees to
disrupt Princess Margaret's visit to Ireland during the
1960s, and also two women. When they left the pub they
were arrested by armed Special Branch detectives, and
Behal and Gallagher were charged with IRA membership.

They were, in effect, holding charges, giving the Gardaí

time to process other charges against Gallagher. He was one of the most wanted men in the country, suspected of involvement in a whole series of operations, including the Donoughmore kidnapping, the Strabane bombing and a number of bank raids. On Sunday, 18 August, three days after his arrest, he was one of nineteen prisoners who blew their way out of Portlaoise Prison using plastic explosives. The coincidence of Gallagher's arrest on the weekend of the breakout saw him credited with a major role in the operation. But, far from being a player in the event – and the man who smuggled in the explosives, as some newspaper reports speculated – his turning up in the area that weekend brought with it a very unwelcome security presence that almost caused the operation to be aborted. According to one IRA source, the escape had to be postponed for a day because of the attention he had attracted.

After the breakout, Gallagher hid for forty-eight hours in a drainage ditch with Kevin Mallon, the commander of the IRA in Tyrone, who would become a central figure in Gallagher's next kidnapping and the main player behind two more in 1983.

❖❖❖

Mallon was thirty-six and a member of the IRA Army Council who had cut his teeth during the Border Campaign of 1956-1962. As a teenager he was acquitted of murdering RUC sergeant Arthur Owens, who was blown to pieces by a mine after he kicked open the door of a disused cottage near Mallon's home in Coalisland. Since the outbreak of the Troubles he had become the leader of the Provisionals in

Tyrone and had become the organisation's most famous escapologist. Portlaoise was the second time he'd broken out of prison in the Republic in the space of ten months.

On 31 October 1973, while serving a sentence for membership, he was plucked from the exercise yard of Mountjoy jail in a hijacked helicopter, along with two other IRA leaders, Seamus Twomey, the former Belfast commander of the Provisionals, and JB O'Hagan, an IRA veteran who was on the Army Council. The operation bore many of the same hallmarks as the Gortahork hijack three months later, though Gallagher's unit probably copied the *modus operandi*. A man who called himself Mr Leonard and who spoke with an American accent had chartered the Alouette Mark II used in the escape from Irish Helicopters, the company that owned the vehicle used in the Strabane bombing. As luck, or rather ill-luck, would have it, the booking was taken by Captain John Hobday, the man who was later forced to fly over the barracks in Tyrone while two milk churn bombs were pushed out. 'Mr Leonard' said he wanted to charter the helicopter to take aerial photographs of the Rock of Dunmaise, an historic outcrop surrounded by ruined walls in the heart of the Laois countryside.

'Mr Leonard' met with the pilot, Captain Robin Thompson Boyce, at one o'clock at Dublin Airport and asked him to fly to Stradbally, County Laois, where a local farmer who had been told the same cover story had given them permission to land. When the helicopter touched down, 'Mr Leonard' got out and a stocky man wearing a mask and carrying a .38 revolver appeared. The pilot was presented with a map and, with the revolver pointing at him, was ordered to fly to

Mountjoy jail, close to Dublin's city centre, and to land in the yard of D wing, the political section. Mallon, Twomey and O'Hagan were walking around the exercise yard together when the helicopter appeared overhead. Using two pieces of paper as directional signals, Mallon waved the helicopter. He boarded first, followed by Twomey and O'Hagan, while prison officers were prevented from reaching them by a cheering mob. It was one of the IRA's most daring raids. The chopper landed on Baldoyle racecourse, north of the city, where the three got away in a taxi that had been hired at Eden Quay and hijacked at gunpoint on its way there. Afterwards the Government decided to move all IRA prisoners out of Mountjoy to a heavy security prison in Portlaoise.

Mallon was picked up again within a matter of weeks of the escape when he was spotted at a dance at a hotel in Portlaoise organised by a local GAA club. When he left the hotel at 2.15am the Gardaí were waiting outside for him. During a brief scuffle, a gun was pulled out but it failed to fire. Marion Coyle, a young woman from Derry, was arrested and charged with attempted murder but was acquitted due to lack of identification evidence. She was set to become Gallagher's partner in the kidnapping that would lead to the biggest manhunt in the history of the State and put them at the top of the Provisionals' own wanted list.

❖❖❖

Being part of the Portlaoise breakout seemed to fire Gallagher's belief that Dugdale too could be sprung from jail. By the end of 1974 he was desperate to get her out. She had given birth to their son, Ruairí, in Limerick jail, where,

Gallagher would later allege in court, she was beaten so severely by warders that the baby was born with two broken arms. Freeing her became an obsession with him. He smuggled a hacksaw blade in to her, which was later discovered during a cell search. According to an IRA source, he was also maintaining contact with her via a two-way radio that had been sneaked in. In April 1975 incendiary devices left in a number of Limerick hotels were linked to an attempt to bring about Dugdale's release.

By then, Gallagher was already plotting another kidnapping and was carrying around a copy of *Who's Who in Ireland*, in which he had placed Xs beside the biographies of eighty different people, all of them leading figures in business, the judiciary, politics or members of the aristocracy. The thickness of each X denoted the size of the prize. But Gallagher had settled on his target almost a year before he eventually took him hostage.

In November 1974, while on the run after the Portlaoise escape, he turned up in Tullamore, County Offaly, where he had many friends and acquaintances. One of them was Brian McGowan, a twenty-year-old motor mechanic and part-time van driver who had been in the IRA for less than a year. During his brief time in Portlaoise, Gallagher had met Brian's brother, Tom, who was in on a membership charge, Gallagher turned up at McGowan's house and they talked for a while before he told him about his plan to get Dugdale out of prison by carrying out a kidnap. McGowan agreed to scout the job for him and Gallagher asked him to find out what he could about a man he was interested in kidnapping.

Tiede Herrema was a wealthy, fifty-four year-old Dutch

industrialist who was chief executive of the Ferenka factory near Annacotty in County Limerick. The factory manufactured steel cord for car tyres and was part of the giant AZKO corporation, one of the largest multinationals in Europe. Gallagher told McGowan that Herrema was an economic – and therefore legitimate – target. And therein lay his gamble. Ferenka was Limerick's biggest employer. Gallagher figured that the Irish government would accede to any ransom demand made for him for fear of the bad publicity damaging foreign investment in the country.

McGowan was given the name and address of an IRA sympathiser who worked at Ferenka. The contact filled him in on where Herrema lived and told him he drove a silver Mercedes. Gallagher said he needed to know more, especially about his movements, so McGowan went back to Limerick, parked outside the factory one evening and then followed Herrema the two miles back to his home on the Monaleen Road. McGowan returned to Tullamore but didn't hear from Gallagher again until well into the New Year.

By then, McGowan, like many republicans, had become disillusioned with the IRA over its ceasefires of 1974 and 1975. After peace talks with Protestant churchmen in Feakle, County Clare, the Provisionals declared a unilateral truce on 22 December 1974. It lasted for twenty-five days and was followed soon after by a second while the leadership took part in secret talks with the British government, convinced that they wanted to pull out of Northern Ireland. But many republicans believed the British would use the truce as a chance to take a breather and improve their intelligence on the IRA before trying to crush them once and for all.

McGowan had almost forgotten about his reconnaissance trips to Limerick by the time Gallagher called to his home again, in January 1975, but he was able to tell him precisely where Herrema lived and what time he left work in the evening. Gallagher said this was no good, as the snatch would have to take place early in the morning. He needed to know what time Herrema left for work. McGowan went back to Limerick, waited at a T-junction on the Monaleen Road and watched Herrema's silver Mercedes pull out of the driveway of the family home at 8.10am. To establish if this was the target's regular routine, he returned again in the middle of February, parked outside the Hurler's Bar on the Monaleen Road and again watched him leave his house just after 8am. After that, McGowan didn't hear from Gallagher for five months and presumed he'd cooled on the whole idea.

❖❖❖

Gallagher was a busy man. On St Patrick's Day he was involved in another dramatic attempted prison break, which saw an IRA prisoner shot dead. Just before 8.30pm on 17 March 1975, six cars were simultaneously set on fire around the town of Portlaoise to create a diversion as an active service unit prepared to drive through the outer prison wall in a lorry and leave with a cargo of prisoners. A heavy steel chain was flung at an ESB transformer, throwing not only the prison into darkness but also most of the town. Only the security lights, which were connected to an army generator, remained on. Seconds after the blackout, the sound of shooting was heard outside the prison, followed by two loud explosions, as a large group of prisoners, using plastic explosives, blew a hole in the wall of the recreation hall, then blasted open a gate in a perimeter fence. They spilled out into an outer compound area, where they waited to be collected by an IRA unit in a lorry that had been covered in reinforced steel. The lorry, with four Volunteers on board, drove through the prison's farm gates and made its way towards the compound. But guards on the roof of the prison opened fire. One prisoner, Thomas Smith, was shot dead as he tried to escape. The lorry didn't make it as far as the compound. Two of the IRA men in the lorry were captured. It's not known whether Gallagher was one of the two who escaped, though he boasted of his involvement in the operation at his eventual trial.

During his time on the run he and his unit also carried out a number of major robberies, which eventually saw him fall foul of the Provisional leadership. The IRA wanted to know where all the money had gone. One newspaper at the time quoted a senior IRA source as saying that Gallagher had a death sentence hanging over him for misappropriating hundreds of thousands of pounds that should have gone into the Provisionals' coffers. The allegation enraged the ideologist Gallagher to the point that he was still railing about it in court a year later, and it was almost certainly without foundation. Gallagher, according to a senior figure from the time, used his cut of the money to finance operations, however foolhardy they often were, and it was another member of the gang who was believed to have been creaming off the money. Nonetheless, their unpredictability had made Gallagher and his friends a dangerous embarrassment for the Provisionals. Gallagher in particular was considered a loose cannon by the leadership and it was decided to run the unit to ground. According to one IRA source:

> It's not true to say there was a death sentence out on him. Look, if they wanted to execute him he'd have to have faced a court martial first. And if you announce that there's a death sentence on someone before they're court martialled, then that's their defence and they get off. No, they wanted to interview him about a few things. There was a robbery on a security van in Meath. There was a post office robbery in Clara. There were quite a few other robberies in the midlands that he was believed to have been behind. Gallagher was using the money to fund the various operations he was doing. He had been getting money from Dugdale. She was independently wealthy. But her money was gone now so he had to start funding himself. There was also a view that it was about time Gallagher was reined in, especially with all the operations he was doing in the Republic with no sanction at all.

But as far as Gallagher was concerned, he was on the run from the IRA as well as the Gardaí. His increasing sense of desperation reawakened his interest in kidnapping. And, despite his initial focus on Herrema, he now appeared to have set his sights on a bigger fish. On Wednesday, 30 April, he and his gang were believed to have been involved in the abduction of the sixty-three-year-old former Lord Colonial Chief Justice, Sir Paget Bourke, from his home in Donnybrook in south Dublin. At 9.15pm Bourke's wife, Susan, answered a knock at the front door and opened it to find two armed men standing there. One put his hand over her mouth and dragged her to the floor. 'Where's Sir Arthur?' she was asked. She said she didn't know who Sir Arthur

Shergar and his owner, the Aga Khan, at the Curragh racecourse

Above: Chief Supt James Murphy from Naas speaking to the press on the Shergar kidnapping

Left: Lord and Lady Donoughmore celebrate their release with Assistant Garda Commissioner Edmund Garvey (standing, left)

Above: Dolours and Marian Price,
whose hungerstrike prompted the
kidnapping of Lord and Lady
Donoughmore
Right: Dr Tiede Herrema

Above: Gardaí at the window of the house in Monasterevin where Herrema was being held

Below: Eddie Gallagher in police custody

Opposite top: Tiede and Elisabeth Herrema leaving Ireland

Opposite below: Ben Dunne and his wife, Mary

Above: The churchyard at Cullyhanna, where Ben Dunne waited to be collected on his release by the kidnappers

Left: Fr Dermod McCarthy, a friend of the Dunnes, holds the three bullets given to Ben Dunne by his captors

> "I know you to be shrewd intelligent men. I appeal to you, in the name of God & in the name of common-sense – cut your losses now, release Ben & get out while you still have time."

Right and above: The appeal that Dermod McCarthy broadcast to the IRA

Below: Don Tidey is reunited with his family after his rescue. (left to right) Andrew, Don, Susan and Alistair

Don Tidey pictured some years after his abduction

was. They seemed to believe that Sir Arthur Galsworthy, the British Ambassador to Ireland, was either visiting the house or possibly even lived there. At that point, Bourke, who had heard voices in the hallway, came out of the living room to see his wife lying face down on the floor, while a man tied her hands behind her back with a necktie. Before he could speak, the other man pushed a gun into his stomach and took him outside to a waiting car.

One man drove while the other sat in the back with the gun pointed at him. They drove for half an hour, then pulled over and the personnel changed. Two new men got in. Like the others, they both seemed to have southern accents. The car headed in a north westerly direction, towards the border. At Ballyconnell they ran into a routine joint Garda and army checkpoint. The driver of the car was asked to present his licence, which he did. Suddenly, Bourke, who thought he was on the Northern side of the border, shouted, 'Soldier! Help!' and the car was forced to break through the checkpoint. A pistol was shoved into his mouth with such force that, he said later, he was surprised his front teeth weren't broken. They drove at speed for a few hundred yards before the men ditched the car and their hostage and escaped across the fields. The Gardaí refused to comment on speculation that the would-be kidnappers intended exchanging their hostage for Dugdale, who was then on hunger strike in protest at conditions in Limerick jail.

❖❖❖

Gallagher returned to his plan to kidnap Herrema, but now the plot involved freeing more than Dugdale. Kevin Mallon

– whose talent for escaping from prison was matched only by his ability to get recaptured just as quickly – had been rearrested at a house in south Dublin earlier in the year. Springing him again, Gallagher figured, would give him an ally at senior level within the IRA and win him immunity from whatever punishment was planned for him. He would take Herrema and demand, in exchange for his life, the release of Dugdale, Mallon and also Jim Hyland, an IRA man from Portlaoise, who had an extensive network of contacts in the midlands and was reputed to know every blade of grass within a twenty-mile radius of Portlaoise prison.

In July 1975, Brian McGowan was surprised to see Gallagher back at his door. Gallagher mentioned the Herrema operation again and asked him to case his house one final time. McGowan did as he was told. It seemed that Herrema was fastidious in his habits. He left the house at the same time every morning. In the meantime, Gallagher enlisted the help of another republican, PJ Bailey, from Monasterevin. A contemporary of his recalls:

PJ wasn't what you would call a serious IRA man, not like his father. Ned Bailey was a Fifties and Sixties man from Portlaoise, a great operator, hugely respected. PJ was really just a gofer. He ran errands. He would have done it for his father at first. But he knew Gallagher. And really it was classic Eddie, the way he would cultivate these contacts. He'd identify people he thought might be able to help him in the future, then he'd cut them away from the herd and work on them. Maybe it wasn't as deliberate as that but it was instinctive with him. That's the way he looked at people. You were either someone who could be of use to him in the future or you weren't. He'd meet you and then one day out of the blue he'd call to your house and tell you he needed a favour, but no one can know about it. So he'd isolate you. He was brilliant at that. Then he'd use you to buy supplies, move arms, hide people, whatever. He always had this network of contacts who'd do favours for him. And PJ was just one of those.

Gallagher decided that they needed two cars for the job: a stolen one, which they would use to snatch Herrema and then dump afterwards, and a regular one, which they could safely use to transport him around, keeping one step ahead of the Garda and army search teams. On 2 September, Gallagher and Bailey went to NA Finlay and Sons in Newbridge and bought a seven-year-old blue Fiat 850 Coupe for £200. Gallagher waited outside while Bailey paid cash for the car, giving his name as John Murphy from Carlow.

Gallagher planned to abduct Herrema around the end of September and waited until close to the date to steal the other car to be used in the job. His vehicle of choice was, as usual, a Ford Cortina, stolen from outside the Grange golf club near Rathfarnham, County Dublin. It was taken to Monasterevin, where it was hidden in a garage and resprayed dark green. False number plates were fitted, along with a new ignition switch, and two steels struts in the back compartment were removed to create a hatch offering access to the boot from the back seat. A week later, Gallagher called to see McGowan again. This time there was a young Derry woman with him, whom he introduced as Marion Coyle. She said very little, but that wasn't out of character for her.

❖❖❖

Coyle was born in July 1954 into a city that was condemned to sectarian division and economic stasis by its unionist leaders. The city's minority Protestant population kept Catholics out of positions of power, while Catholic families were shoehorned into the unemployment ghetto of the Bogside to prevent a shift in the thin voting balances in the city's gerrymandered electoral wards.

Coyle had an outwardly atypical upbringing for a Derry republican. She grew up in a smart, semi-detached house on Duncreggan Road in one of the more fashionable parts of the city, about a mile from the Bogside. Her parents, Johnnie and Susan Coyle, were well-known shopkeepers in the Creggan and her birth in what Catholics celebrated as the Marian Year made her name a natural choice for their sixth of ten children. She was a striking-looking young woman, petite with prominent cheekbones and penetrating eyes. At sixteen, she enrolled in the Municipal Technical College to learn shorthand, typing and advanced English. She was a quiet teenager, showing none of the qualities that would make her one of the IRA's most fearless and respected Volunteers and the woman Gallagher described as 'the greatest and bravest soldier I've ever worked with'.

She experienced a political awakening in the maelstrom of the early Troubles, as the collapse of civil power brought her city to its knees. When it all started it Derry in 1968 she still too young to appreciate what was happening or the way in which it would shape her life. The Vietnam War protests in America and Britain, the Paris Uprising and the

Prague spring that year had made street protest fashionable as a means of expressing mass dissent, and in Northern Ireland, middle-class students took to the streets to protest against the unionist stranglehold on power. The Stormont Government overreacted. On 5 October 1968, in defiance of a ban, four hundred members of the Northern Ireland Civil Rights Association took part in a march. When they reached the Protestant Waterside district, they were trapped between two police cordons and the RUC waded into the crowd with their heavy batons. The modern Troubles had begun.

In January 1969 a march by forty members of the radical left-wing People's Democracy was attacked by a loyalist mob at Burntollet Bridge near Derry. Marchers were attacked with bottles, bricks and lengths of wood, while RUC officers stood back and watched. Fierce sectarian rioting broke out in the city that summer and the conflagration spread to Belfast, where 1,500 Catholic and 300 Protestant families were driven from their homes by sectarian mobs. From the anarchic vacuum the IRA emerged as the self-declared defenders of the Catholic community. Exhausted, the RUC conceded defeat and British Home Secretary James Callaghan ordered troops in to restore order.

The arrival of the soldiers was greeted as a victory by the Bogsiders, but relations between them quickly soured. The army soon came to see them as the problem and they came to see the army as a force of occupation. To nationalists, the soldiers were just as keen perpetrators of assaults, provocation and fabrication of evidence as the RUC. The army killing in July 1971 of twenty-eight-year-old Seamus Cusack and nineteen-year-old Desmond Beattie, both of whom were unarmed, is credited for the birth of the Provisionals in the city. Six months later, the Parachute Regiment opened fire on a civil rights march in Derry, shooting dead fourteen unarmed men. It was the seminal moment in the explosion of the Troubles. An editorial in the following day's *Irish Press* said presciently: 'If there was an able bodied man with republican sympathies within Derry who was not in the IRA before yesterday's butchery, there will be none tonight.'

But the event that probably had the biggest impact on Coyle happened earlier, in the summer of 1970, the year she enrolled in the local technical college. On 26 June, the civil rights MP, Bernadette Devlin, was arrested at a roadblock on her way to address a meeting at Free Derry Corner. Her appeal against a six-month sentence for her part in the rioting in the Bogside the previous summer had been dismissed and she had arranged to be 'arrested by appointment' after addressing the meeting. The news of her arrest provoked some of the most serious rioting yet. A dense black fog hung over the city as shops and business premises were burned to the ground. The army, pelted with stones and petrol bombs, fired 1,300 canisters of CS gas to try to bring order.

That night, Coyle's uncle Joe died, along with the rest of the middle echelon of the Provisional leadership in the city, when a bomb they were making blew up in their faces. They were preparing the device in the kitchen of the home of Tommy McCool, a veteran of the Border Campaign, in the Creggan Estate. A short time after midnight there was an explosion. Coyle and McCool died on the scene. Another Volunteer, Thomas Carlin, died later in hospital. The explosion also killed two of McCool's young daughters, Bernardette and Carol, who became officially the first female victims of the Troubles.

The poorly led Provisionals had little support in the city until the emergence of Martin McGuinness, the so-called boy general of the Derry IRA, in the wake of the Cusack and Beattie killings. It was difficult to remain impartial in the city after Bloody Sunday. Phillip, the brother Marion was closest to, served time in prison for possessing a gun. Marion herself was nineteen when she chalked up her first arrest. She and four others were stopped at a checkpoint in Sligo and the car in which they were travelling was found to contain guns and ammunition. Among the others arrested – two men and two women – was Leo Martin from Belfast, the reported OC of the Northern IRA, who took the rap for the arms cache. In 1974 she escaped jail again when she was acquitted of the attempted murder of a Garda during Kevin Mallon's arrest in Portlaoise. Within the IRA she had developed a reputation as a fearless and professional operative. According to one Volunteer who worked with her:

> She was excellent. First class. A total no-shit merchant. It was always, 'What's the operation? What's my part?' and that was it. She said very little. She was very cool. There was huge respect for her in the IRA. Martin McGuinness would have thought the world of her, especially with her family background. There would have been a lot of surprise in Derry when it came out that she was operating with Gallagher but the thing about the Herrema job was that the justification for it was in its success. If it had worked, they would have been heroes, and she understood that. The truth, though, is

that she was in love with Mallon. I'm not saying it was ever reciprocated, but she had this infatuation with him, as a lot of women did. He was a very charismatic man. I remember being at meetings and the word would go round that Mallon was on his way and the women would get all excited. Marion had this fascination with Mallon, and Gallagher was no fool. He'd have known how to use that. He was very manipulative.

❖❖❖

Gallagher, Coyle and McGowan met at Tommy Dolan's pub in Clara, County Offaly, to make their final preparations for the abduction. Gallagher and Coyle sat drinking brandies while McGowan drew them a plan of the road where Herrema lived, indicating the house. Gallagher asked him about traffic in the area and McGowan said it was very light. Gallagher was driving the Fiat Coupe that he and Bailey had bought in Newbridge. He was unhappy with it. It turned out to be too small for the job and he asked McGowan to look after it, making sure to run the engine regularly just in case it was needed. Gallagher and Coyle dropped the car off to him the following day and left in the stolen Cortina. McGowan parked the Fiat at the back of a neighbour's house.

He was given one more job. He was asked to find a safe house somewhere in the midlands where they could hold Herrema once they'd snatched him. He called to the home of a friend who'd helped put up men on the run in the past. McGowan was introduced to David Dunne, a sixty-three-year-old small farmer who lived with his elderly, semi-invalid mother in a single-storey cottage in Mountmellick,

County Laois. He was asked if he would 'take a few fellas for a few days' and he agreed, though it's doubtful if he knew quite what he was getting involved in. Dunne's sympathies were unknown to the Gardaí and he had come to their attention only once, twenty-five years before, when he intervened to stop three men beating up a Garda and was commended by a circuit court judge in Portlaoise.

In the meantime, Gallagher had also recruited Vincent Walsh, a twenty-six year-old bricklayer from Derrygolan, just north of Tullamore, County Offaly. He was entrusted with the job of finding safe houses for Dugdale, Mallon and Hyland once they'd been sprung from jail, though he would also help with the abduction itself. The team's base of operations was an isolated farmhouse in Kinnity, not far from Birr, in the sparsely populated foothills of the Slieve Bloom Mountains. With its dense forests and narrowing, snaking roads, it was one of Gallagher's favourite boltholes during his time on the run. On the night of 29 September 1975, in the kitchen of the house, the gang finalised their plans to drive to Limerick and snatch Herrema the following morning. They went to bed, Coyle in the spare room and Gallagher, McGowan and Walsh in sleeping bags on the living room floor.

Gallagher's alarm clock went off at 5am. They got up, checked their arsenal – two Czech Vzor .32 pistols and two Smith and Wesson .38 revolvers – and were on the road an hour later. The plan to pick Herrema up was straightforward. Coyle would wait in the grounds of the church almost opposite the house and use a two-way radio to signal to the others as soon as his car turned out of the driveway. Gallagher, McGowan and Walsh would wait for the car in a gateway two hundred yards down the road. Gallagher was wearing a postman's uniform with badges sewn onto it to pass himself off as a Garda. He would flag down Herrema's car, drag him out at gunpoint, bundle him into the stolen Cortina and spirit him off to the safe house in Mountmellick, before demanding the prisoner releases. By the gang's estimation, the abduction itself would take less than sixty seconds.

They took their positions and waited for Herrema's silver Mercedes to appear. By nine o'clock there was still no sign of it. They wondered if he had gone to work earlier than usual that morning and they drove to the factory to see if they could see his car in the carpark. There was no sign of it. They drove back to Kinnity and spent the rest of the day playing cards and talking. The following morning they went back, but again Herrema's car failed to appear. It was the same story the morning after that. Then they realised what had happened. Herrema had loaned his regular car to a colleague and had been passing them every morning in a Hillman Hunter estate car that belonged to the company. So, on Friday, 3 October 1975, after three false starts, they set off from Kinnity at six o'clock in the morning, McGowan driving, Coyle in the front passenger seat, Gallagher and Walsh sitting in the back, knowing that this time it was happening for real.

❖❖❖

As he got into his car, Tiede Herrema's mind was on a potentially difficult meeting that morning with US and Dutch businessmen. His son, Harm, opened the garage door for him and closed it when he'd gone. Herrema said, 'See you later,' before disappearing down the driveway and out onto the Monaleen Road. Coyle, wearing large tinted glasses and a scarf, stood in the church grounds and tried to radio ahead to the others when Herrema passed. The radio didn't work, but Gallagher was ready anyway. Halfway down the Monaleen Road, Herrema saw what he took to be a Garda standing in the middle of the road. He stopped and wound down his window. Gallagher approached the driver's door and asked him his name. 'Doctor Herrema,' he repied. Gallagher drew a revolver, pointed it at his head and shouted, 'Come out of the fucking car'. He tore open the door and dragged Herrema out just as McGowan pulled up alongside them in the Cortina. Herrema was pushed into the back of the car, between Gallagher and Walsh, who, like McGowan, had the lower half of his face covered. They put tape over his eyes, picked Coyle up and headed for the main Limerick to Dublin road.

At the time of the kidnap the Ferenka plant was paralysed by an industrial dispute, the latest of many that took place at the factory. The fitters had gone on an unofficial strike over the factory's failure to honour the national wage agreement. At first, Herrema believed his four captors were disgruntled employees who were trying to frighten him. Then Gallagher asked him for the name of someone in the German embassy in Dublin. Herrema was thrown by the question. 'I'm not from Germany,' he said. 'I'm a Dutchman.'

This exchange could hold the key to one of the enduring mysteries of the kidnapping: why Gallagher and Coyle considered Herrema to be such a big prize. The reference to

Germany may have been just a slip of the tongue in the frantic, adrenalin-charged minutes after the snatch. But if Gallagher really did believe Herrema was German, it could explain why he chose him as a target. He may have considered the Germans to be weak in the face of hostage-related blackmail. In October 1972 they released three Palestinian terrorists who took part in the Munich Olympics massacre after two members of Black September, armed with pistols and hand grenades, hijacked a Lufthansa Boeing 727 over Turkey. Gallagher may have believed the German government would exert pressure on Liam Cosgrave to save the life of one of its citizens. Or maybe it was just a mistake.

He asked Herrema who he knew in the Dutch embassy and Herrema told him he was on speaking terms with the ambassador to Ireland, Felix von Raalte. Gallagher also asked whether production at Ferenka would be halted if Herrema gave the instruction, and he said he believed it would. They drove on. Sitting in darkness, Herrema tried to figure out which direction they were headed from his sense of the sun's position in the sky. He guessed, rightly, that they were travelling in a north easterly direction. They took the Dublin road as far as Annacotty, then turned east and drove through Nenagh and Roscrea before reaching the farmhouse in Kinnity at about 9.30am.

Herrema, still blindfolded, was taken out of the car and made to sit down on a bundle of hay. A coat was put over his head. He knew he was on a farm because he could hear cows. He sat there for ten minutes while the gang organised themselves. McGowan, who had arrived in the Fiat, took it back to Tullamore. Herrema was put back into the Cortina and soon they were moving again. He could tell from the way the car was being driven that the driver had changed. Coyle had taken the wheel, while Gallagher and Walsh sat on either side of him in the back. They took the road through Cadamstown and rounded the northern side of the Slieve Blooms to reach the house in Mountmellick by 10.15am.

David Dunne was there when they arrived. According to his own account, he only realised the seriousness of what he'd got involved in when he saw Gallagher and Coyle frog-marching a man with a hood over his head into the house. Later that day he heard about the kidnapping on the news and it dawned on him that the man the Gardaí were looking for was tied up in his spare room. He went to Gallagher and asked him whether he planned to kill the man. Gallagher said no and added that he only shot informers. Dunne took it as a warning.

Coyle dropped Walsh back to Tullamore so he could get ready for his next job, which was to hide the three prisoners when they were released. At 11.30am she phoned the Dutch embassy and said she was involved in the kidnapping that morning of the industrialist, Tiede Herrema, news of which had not yet reached the media. She said they were demanding the release of three republican prisoners – Rose Dugdale, Kevin Mallon and James Hyland – and that if they weren't freed within forty-eight hours then Herrema would be executed. As an act of good faith, she demanded that the Ferenka factory be closed for twenty-four hours and that the Gardaí refrain from mounting roadblocks or searches. Again, failure to comply would result in Herrema's death. When Coyle felt the call had lasted almost long enough to enable a trace, she hung up and phoned back five minutes later to repeat the message. Then she phoned the *Irish Press* in Dublin and asked to be put through to the newsroom. She coolly repeated what she'd told the Dutch embassy. After that she drove the stolen Cortina to Dublin and abandoned it in Parkgate Street, close to the spot in the Phoenix Park where Lord and Lady Donoughmore had been released.

In the meantime, Herrema had been placed in a small bedroom where car parts cluttered the floor. Gallagher decided the room wasn't suitable and moved him to a smaller one. Herrema was still blindfolded and cotton wool had been placed in his ears and taped over. His wrists and ankles were also bound. Some time that afternoon Gallagher removed the tape from Herrema's eyes and ears to explain to him why he'd been kidnapped. Then he produced a portable tape recorder with a microphone and handed Herrema a statement that he'd written out on a piece of paper. He wanted him to read it out. Gallagher hit the 'record' button and Herrema did what he was told, although it took several recitals before he got it word perfect.

The statement addressed the Dutch ambassador to Ireland. It said: 'Mr von Raalte, this is Herrema. This well-organised group is going to jeopardise the position of Ferenka in Limerick forever and you know how important Ferenka is to the development of Limerick and Ireland. Please put pressure on the Government – the Dutch and Irish governments – to get me free and let the Irish government answer the demands of this group, who are very serious. Seeing the situation I am in, my condition is reasonable.

Love to my wife and children. Workers of Ferenka, keep the factory closed till I am free or till you hear from me. Don't put pressure on the group who abducted me. It may be better to put pressure on the Government to save Ferenka.'

When the recording was finished, Herrema asked what would happen if the demands weren't met. Gallagher said that in that case he'd have only forty-eight hours to live, but he seemed confident that it wouldn't come to that.

❖❖❖

The Government was informed before lunchtime. The minister for justice, Paddy Cooney, remembers being passed a note at the regular Friday morning meeting of the Cabinet, telling him that a Dutch businessman had been kidnapped and that the ransom was the release of three IRA prisoners. Everyone around the table agreed that they would stand by their pact not to do any deals. 'What they are asking is that we open the gates and let subversive criminals loose in society with immunity,' Cooney said that day. 'People whose organisation wants to bring down the institutions of this State. The Government has no choice in this matter. The position we adopt is a simple one politically, although from an emotional and psychological point of view, with a man's life at stake, it is difficult. This stunt is absolutely futile.'

Security at Limerick Prison, where Dugdale was held, was intensified on Cooney's instructions; the walls sand-bagged, new observation posts set up on the prison walls and dozens of extra Gardaí and armed soldiers placed on round-the-clock duty. At lunchtime the Government received an important break when the IRA disassociated itself from the kidnapping, pulling the carpet from under Gallagher and Coyle. It said: 'We have been asked to state that neither the Republican movement or any of its members had an involvement in the kidnapping of Mr Herrema. Further, it is not the policy of the Republican movement to differentiate between Republican prisoners in seeking their release.'

The Dutch prime minister, Dr Joop den Uyl, sent a message to Cooney, asking him to do everything he could to save Herrema. There were reports that political pressure was exerted on the Government by the Dutch to negotiate for his life, but according to Cooney:

> The Netherlands Government put no pressure (on us) whatever to deal with Dr Herrema's kidnappers and no telegram in that regard was sent to us ... Their ambassador was regularly briefed by me and I did many interviews with the Dutch media to reassure the Dutch public that we had the resources and the competence to deal with the matter. We were new members of the then EEC and little enough was known about Ireland on the Continent.

The Gardaí issued a description of Dr Herrema: five feet ten inches tall, thin build, athletic appearance, sallow complexion, receding hairline, sharp features, wearing a grey suit, white shirt and black shoes. The joint army and Garda search got underway that afternoon and within a week four thousand Gardaí – half the total force – were involved in the hunt for the kidnappers across more than ten counties.

But the most significant breakthrough in the case came almost immediately when the Gardaí threw their dragnets over known republicans in the midlands, where Gallagher had been seen recently. At 1.30pm, just two hours after the ransom demand was issued, Detective John Durcan and Sergeant John Halloran called to McGowan's home in Tullamore. McGowan wasn't home, but in a caravan at the back of the house they found Walsh listening to the lunchtime news. He was understandably surprised to find the Gardaí on their trail so quickly. He was asked to account for his movements that morning. He toughed it out. He was at home for most of the morning, he said. He was unemployed and had no reason to get up early. He left home in the middle of the morning and went into town at around eleven o'clock. Durcan and Halloran left, convinced that Walsh knew more than he let on.

McGowan needed an alibi. On the night of the kidnapping, John Magee was in Martin Moran's pub in Kilbeggan, County Wesmeath, when McGowan came in just before closing time. The two knew each other well. McGowan asked him what he'd been doing all day and Magee said he'd been busy in his workshop. McGowan told him that if the Gardaí came asking questions about him he was to say he'd been working with him all day.

❖❖❖

After dumping the Cortina in Dublin, Coyle spent the night with a friend in the city and went back to Mountmellick the following day, Saturday. When she got there, Herrema's room was in complete darkness. The windows were boarded up and the curtains were closed. But he wasn't completely cut off from what was happening; there was a radio in the other room and he could hear it through the door. He listened to the news, which had reports of where the searches were concentrated, and he wondered how far away they were. Occasionally, a helicopter passed overhead, giving him some hope that the Gardaí might find him.

For the rest of the time he concentrated on staying sane. Tied up, blindfolded and imprisoned in a small, darkened room, he maintained his mental equilibrium by living out his daily routine in his imagination, a trick he'd learned as a psychology student. He slept only at night and filled the daylight hours by sticking to his regular schedule in his mind. In the morning he imagined himself washing and shaving. Then he ate a big breakfast. Just after 8am he left the house and drove to Ferenka. He pictured himself working. Then after a big lunch he imagined an hour of exercise. He recalls:

> One of the most important things you learn in studying psychology is how very important it is to keep human standards. It is important that you do not lose contact with normality, no matter where you are. You have to stop yourself from being disorientated. So I tried to live a normal life, even if my situation was not very normal.

Even at fifty-four, Herrema was better equipped to survive a prolonged hostage drama than his kidnappers. During the Second World War he served time as a prisoner of war in Czechoslovakia during the Nazi occupation. He later saw invading Russian soldiers shoot dead a row of innocent people, an incident that had a profound effect on him and which he still refuses to speak about. Physically he was in prime condition. He played tennis, enjoyed ice-skating and had recently shocked Ferenka employees by beating all comers in a 500m race at the factory's sports day. Mentally he was also in robust shape. He was a formidable figure in the boardroom and in his spare time he played chess and had a voracious appetite for books.

Like Gallagher, Herrema had left school early. He trained as a mechanic, but after the war enrolled in a number of part-time university courses, earning a degree in psychology and later a masters degree in arts and philosophy. He joined the giant AKZO multinational in 1954 and steadily climbed the career ladder until his appointment as chief executive of the group's steel cord manufacturing plant in Limerick in 1973. The job was considered a poisoned chalice. The factory had a long and unhappy history of industrial relations problems and there were constant rumours of impending closure because of the recession in the motor industry. Harold O'Sullivan, the prominent trade union official who would play a bit-part role in the negotiations for Herrema's life, says:

> Ferenka weren't competent employers. What happened was they came to Limerick and they set up an awfully laborious, dirty industry that might have worked in a fully industrialised town. But Limerick was not industrialised. So straight away they had a labour shortage problem. So they got guys in from the farms to work in this tedious, dirty atmosphere – this dirty, noisy place – and these guys had never any experience of working in industry in their lives. But they all still had half jobs back on the farm. So they could tell the company to go and … whatever. Let's go out on strike. Even the novelty of being on strike was great because here they were living in two worlds, one as members of the IFA (Irish Farmer's

Association) and farmers and the other as members of a separate trade union and workers in Ferenka. So the company got the worst of all possible worlds. They recruited more people than they could manage properly and then they didn't manage them properly. They were advised not to do it by the union, what is now SIPTU, but they went ahead.

Herrema's posting to Ireland meant breaking up the family. His wife, Elisabeth, a former town councillor in Arnhem, came to Limerick with him, but two of their four children who were in their mid twenties stayed behind in the Netherlands. Despite the difficulty of the job, he warmed to Ireland, loved the countryside and developed a fascination for hurling. He was regarded as a fair-minded boss, whose popularity was reflected in a march by workers through the streets of Limerick. Senior executives at AZKO decided to close the factory for twenty-four hours in line with Gallagher's demands. This was against the advice of Gardaí, who argued that it would raise the kidnappers' hopes of more concessions. Many of the 1,200 staff who brought the centre of the city to a halt were worried for their jobs, but speaker after speaker called for their boss's release.

The Government believed that pressure from the IRA was more likely to bring an end to the kidnapping. Thady Coughlan, the Lord Mayor of Limerick, figured that if the Provisionals were prepared to disassociate themselves from it, then the prisoners themselves would denounce it too, thereby rendering the whole operation pointless. Dugdale refused to see him when he called to Limerick prison on Saturday afternoon. But, taking his lead, Dr Hugh Krayenhoff, the chairman of AZKO, decided to put together a delegation to go to Portlaoise prison to try to get Mallon and Hyland to condemn the kidnapping. According to one IRA source from the time:

> The last thing Jim (James Hyland) wanted was to be sprung. He only had something like a year left. When you're going to be out that soon you just want to keep your nose clean. But he knew the area where Gallagher was hiding out so well, especially around The Heath, and he just served Gallagher's purposes. I'm not sure about Mallon. He didn't do jail well. I think he'd have done anything to get out.

Krayenhoff put together a team, the most important member of which was Reverend William Arlow, secretary of the Irish Council of Churches, who knew Mallon from the talks at Feakle that had brought about the IRA's 1974 and 1975 ceasefires. Paddy Cooney was enthusiastic about the plan and gave permission for the visit. On Sunday morning, Arlow was flown from Belfast to Dublin in a company jet, then taken in a smaller plane to a field near the Curragh, from where he was driven under heavy Garda escort to the prison. The IRA wanted former chief of staff Joe Cahill at the talks, but Cooney wouldn't allow it and Robert Smith, a close ally of Cahill, was put up instead.

Arlow, Krayenhoff and Smith met Mallon and Hyland in an interview room, but that was as far as they got. Mallon wanted the talks governed by normal visiting procedures, with a prison warder present but out of earshot. But Willie O'Reilly, the prisoner governor, insisted on being in the room. The two prisoners walked out. While disappointed, the Government publicly defended O'Reilly's actions on 'security grounds'. Mallon had, after all, escaped from Port-laoise before and from another prison in the State. The delegation found themselves putting forward conditions under which talks might take place. In the end they gave up.

❖❖❖

David Dunne was scared. The kidnapping was dominating the television and radio news and he was struggling with guilt. Gallagher had put him in charge of Herrema's meals. It was usually potatoes and meat for dinner, followed by homemade apple pie with custard, or at other times, sago. He gave him large helpings, with extra meat, to help the prisoner keep his strength up, but it did nothing to salve his conscience. He went to Confession and told a priest, who advised him to go to the Gardaí. Dunne remembered what Gallagher had said about informers and was too frightened to take that step.

On Sunday night, two days after Herrema's abduction, the Gardaí caught up with McGowan. He claimed under questioning that he had been in bed until ten o'clock on the morning of the kidnapping, had had breakfast, then thumbed a lift to Kilbeggan, County Westmeath, where he had helped his friend, John Magee, dig a pit in his garage. He had dinner there and then returned to Tullamore. He was asked whether he knew Eddie Gallagher or Marion Coyle. He said no. Detective Sergeant Durcan went to check his alibi. He called twice to Magee's home on the Dublin Road, but he wasn't there. The following morning McGowan was released.

At about the same time, a white, unstamped envelope containing a cassette arrived at the Dutch embassy on Merrion Road in Dublin. On it was the prepared statement that Herrema had been made to read out on Friday afternoon in Mountmellick. The sound quality was poor, a cacophony of background noise and crackles, but the message was clear. The envelope and cassette were sent for forensic testing. On the envelope they found a palm print that belonged to Eddie Gallagher.

On Tuesday, 7 October, the search was stepped up in the areas Gallagher was known to frequent. Five hundred soldiers from Collins Barracks, backed by Garda recruits, combed the foothills of the Slieve Blooms, searching houses and barns in the area, while helicopters ferried troops to the top of the mountain to pick their way through vast areas of remote scrubland. Their rotors could be heard from the house.The searchers were too close for comfort and Gallagher and Coyle decided to move the 'lad', as they had taken to calling Dr Herrema.

The decision to leave Mountmellick may have been taken earlier, Herrema believes, after his complaints about the conditions in which he was being kept. He appealed to his captors' view of themselves as soldiers by threatening to make a complaint to the International Red Cross about the conditions, which he told them were contrary to the Geneva Convention for the Treatment of Prisoners. His room was dirty. There were fleas in his bed. His hands and feet were bound too tightly and he was denied basic sanitation facilities, forced to defecate and urinate in an earthenware pot. It was worse than the prisoner of war camp he had survived, he told Gallagher. That night, Coyle loosened his fetters to give him greater freedom of movement and he was given permission to remove the mask from his eyes when she and Gallagher were not in the room. He was allowed to wash and shave for the first time, to cross the landing to go to the bathroom, and was given permission to do between twenty and thirty minutes of exercise a day, although he had to remain on the bed to do it. Herrema remembers:

> They said they were soldiers. They were fighting for the freedom of Ireland. That's what they kept saying. So I used that. I said if they were soldiers then I was entitled to the proper treatment you expect as a prisoner of war. They changed their attitude towards me.

Gallagher leaned on his midlands contacts to try to find him a new safe house. At lunchtime on Wednesday, a report on the radio said that a capuchin priest, Reverend Donal O'Mahony, was offering to act as a mediator. O'Mahony was the Irish chaplain of Pax Christi, the international peacekeeping movement, and had brokered reconciliation talks in Poland, East Germany and Czechoslovakia. Gallagher and Coyle decided to use him, not as a go-between, but as a mouthpiece to bring public pressure on the Government to do a deal.

That afternoon, Gallagher took the tape recorder into Herrema's room and gave him another, much longer, message to read out. It included a first reference to the Irish Liberation Organisation, which Gallagher and Coyle had resorted to calling themselves since the IRA cut them adrift. Gallagher was furious about a Sunday newspaper report the previous weekend that accused him of enriching himself through a series of armed robberies and wanted to make the point. McGowan was given the tape and told to drop it through the letterbox of a presbytery in Tullamore. At three o'clock in the morning the parish priest, Father John O'Reilly, was phoned to say that a package that had been put through his door was to be passed on to a priest who would be calling the following day. O'Mahony also received a call at the friary on Church Street in Dublin, telling him about the tape. He drove to Tullamore the following morning and listened to the recording in a room on his own.

A man, speaking in a halting voice and with broken English said: 'Father O'Mahony, the organisation who have abducted me is called the Irish Liberation Organisation. They have carried out various bombing missions in England over the last three years. They have told me that their association with the Provisionals only extends to organising escapes from State and English prisons, the last being the Portlaoise armoured car attempt on St Patrick's Day, when Free State soldiers shot an unarmed prisoner.

'They have told me to state that one source from which various slanderous statements which the papers have carried about men in their organisation has been traced. The people responsible will be punished as any informer would be punished. They are not interested in money, nor does adverse publicity bother them.

'So the only way my life can be saved is by everyone putting pressure on the Government to release the three political prisoners named. One of them is the mother of a very young child. Surely if these three people do not leave the country, the secret police can easily arrest them after my life has been spared.

'I must advise AZKO to close Ferenka for the time being. I don't know where I am. My eyes are blinded by tape. My hands and feet are tied and my ears are full of cotton wool. Please get the International Red Cross to plead for my life with the Irish government.

'My abductors are heavily armed and they say they will not give the Irish government the satisfaction of getting me back alive and will use me as a hostage if the secret police discover where I am being held. I've tried to help Ireland. Surely the Irish government will now help me. I ask them for my life.

'My codeword is Tornado Sailing Boat. Indicate that you have got this message. The above message has to be broadcast in full on radio, Thursday, 8pm to 12pm. If the Irish government don't agree, this will absolutely be the last message they give.'

The message was broadcast on Thursday night as demanded. At around the same time, workers who arrived for the late shift at Ferenka were told by security staff that the factory was closed until further notice. On Friday morning, one week after Herrema's abduction, O'Mahony was asked if he thought his release would come soon. 'It's hard to know if it's any nearer now,' he said. 'Certainly his life is still at great risk.'

The searches were continuing in and around Slieve Bloom. If the kidnappers stayed in Mountmellick another weekend they'd be found. PJ Bailey was put on the job. His wife, Bridie, suggested they hide Herrema in a cottage her parents owned in Kildangan, County Kildare. It was a small, thatched house on the Athy Road, shielded from view by a large hedge. On the night of Saturday, 11 October, they dressed Herrema up in a long coat and hat, took him from his room and hustled him, still blindfolded, into the back of a car. Gallagher was dressed as a priest. Coyle drove. They reached Kildangan half an hour early and left Herrema standing in a wooden shed at the back of the house while they waited for the Baileys to arrive with the keys.

Bridie opened up while PJ stayed in the car with their children. Herrema was brought in and put sitting on a bed. There was some argument then between Gallagher, Coyle and Bridie about whether the house was suitable. Coyle was unhappy with it because it had no indoor bathroom. They needed something better. Bridie said that as a last resort she could ask her brother, Michael Hall, a fitter with Irish Ropes in Kildare, whether they could use the spare room of his house in Monasterevin.

Bridie cooked dinner for everyone before PJ drove the forty-five minute drive to Hall's house at 1410 St Evin's Park, a council estate just outside the town. Michael and his wife, Catherine, were in bed when PJ called to the house after midnight. The Halls later claimed in court that they were asked to put up a priest and a girl for the night and knew nothing of PJ and Bridie's connection with the Herrema kidnapping. Catherine prepared a bed while Michael Hall and Bridie Bailey drove to Kildangan to pick up Gallagher, Coyle and Herrema.

Coyle walked out to the car first, carrying an overnight bag containing their kidnapping kit – the cassette recorder, a pair of binoculars, nine buff envelopes, two walkie-talkies, a roll of adhesive tape and Gallagher's copy of *Who's Who in Ireland*, as well as eight watches with the hour hand missing, for use in bombmaking. Gallagher, still in his priest's garb, led Herrema to the car. It was 2.30am when they reached St Evin's Park. Herrema had his blindfold removed, and, with Gallagher pointing his gun at him, was told to walk into the house as normally as possible. He did what he was told and was blindfolded again and put into the boxroom.

Catherine Hall later claimed in court that on her way out to mass on Sunday morning she met Gallagher at the top of the stairs and told him she wasn't happy with what was going on. Gallagher, she claimed, pointed his gun at her and told her to carry on as normal or he'd blow her head off. She said she went downstairs to the living-room and saw Coyle standing in front of the fireplace with a pistol in her hand.

Herrema's conditions improved from the moment he was taken to St Evin's Park. He was treated, in his own words, like one of the family. He was brought a boiled egg and toast for breakfast, ham and tomatoes for lunch and meat with vegetables and potatoes for dinner. He was allowed to visit the bathroom. His blindfold was removed. He read, played chess by himself and continued to go through the motions of a normal day in his mind. He also tried to strike up a relationship with the kidnappers, believing it would make it more difficult for them to kill him if it came to it. He was successful with Gallagher, who watched him during the day while polishing his long-barrelled Smith and Wesson revolver of which he seemed particularly proud. Coyle, who sat guard at night, never spoke to him except to say, 'Here,' when she handed him food or, 'Shut up,' when he tried to engage her in conversation. According to Herrema:

I didn't see Marion Coyle at all in Mountmellick because I was blindfolded there. In total I think it was nine or ten days before I saw her face. She was very pretty. I was quite surprised by how young she was. I had children who were older than she was. But I couldn't reach her. I just got little remarks, like telling me to be quiet. In certain ways I think she was afraid of me. She knew I was getting control of the situation the longer it went on. I had in the back of my mind a plan to build a relationship with them. I started to ask Eddie Gallagher about his background, where he was from, his parents, his brothers and sisters. We would talk for hours. We discussed Communism, industrialisation, politics. We would have these debates. He didn't have very much school education but he was a very intelligent man.

❖❖❖

Gallagher decided to sack Reverend O'Mahony as a mediator after his press conference the previous Friday. It was thought that he'd spent far too much time publicly pleading for Herrema's release for Gallagher's liking, instead of pleading with the Government to do a deal. But there were other reasons why the priest was suddenly considered surplus to requirements. It had dawned on Gallagher that he held no cards. The Government wasn't going to budge no matter how many times they said they were going to shoot Herrema. So unmoved was Cosgrave by their threats that he'd gone to Rome for nine days for the canonisation of Oliver Plunkett, a seventeenth-century priest who was the last Catholic executed for his faith in England and the first Irishman to be made a saint in almost 700 years. Gallagher and Coyle wanted out. All that remained was how much money they could extort from Herrema's employers in exchange for his life. Gallagher had started asking him about various AZKO officials he'd seen on television or quoted in the newspapers. When Herrema told him, early on in Monasterevin, 'I don't think you can win this game, Eddie,' it prompted a discussion about what he figured he was worth to Ferenka. Gallagher's guess was £3m. Herrema said he didn't think it was that much. Gallagher suggested £2m. Herrema said he didn't think they'd pay that either.

The second reason the priest was no longer needed was that Gallagher had been in touch with Phil Flynn, the man who had driven the Donoughmores to freedom. Officially, Flynn's role as a mediator in the Herrema kidnapping didn't begin until Sunday, 12 October, the weekend of the move to Monasterevin, but in fact, Flynn was involved much earlier and had a secret face-to-face meeting with Gallagher the previous weekend, just a couple of days after Herrema was snatched. The meeting took place in the home of a priest not far from Monasterevin itself and followed a phone call from PJ Bailey. Gallagher wanted to involve Flynn for three reasons: he was a skilled negotiator, with good political connections, who might persuade the Government to do a deal on the prisoner releases; he was a proud republican who would take an adversarial stand with Cosgrave and would try to embarrass him at his press conferences; and, as a highly respected figure within the republican movement, he could keep the IRA off his back. But Flynn was loath to stick his neck out for Gallagher again. Helping him could get him into serious trouble with the IRA, not to mention the Gardaí. He told him he needed to think about it and to sound out some of his contacts. In the meantime, Gallagher and Coyle decided they could use O'Mahony and took him up on his offer. But, later in the week, when Flynn got word to them that he'd do it, they no longer needed him.

On Monday, 13 October, Flynn got up early and drove to Monasterevin, but failed to see Gallagher. PJ Bailey told him to go home and that there'd be a phone call at 7.30pm. But first he needed to absent himself from work for the week, so he drove to the Custom House in Dublin to talk to his boss, Harold O'Sullivan, the general secretary of the Local Government and Public Services Union. 'I was on my way to a meeting in Denmark when Phil arrived and asked me to come outside and talk to him,' O'Sullivan remembers.

> He explained the situation of the kidnap to me. Phil himself wasn't that keen on getting involved, but he wanted to get my consent. I said he should do it. As it happened, Herrema was an official of a multinational that didn't cover themselves in a great deal of glory down in Limerick. Nevertheless, he was a human being at some risk, and I didn't see that he had any choice in the matter. I didn't know anything about Phil's relationship with Sinn Féin, the IRA, whatever. But that was an ambivalent time, politically and every other way. And as far as I was concerned, we weren't dealing with a political situation, it was a criminal one. I told Phil, as my assistant, that he could regard himself as free to engage in the rescue of this man in any manner or means he thought appropriate and I, in turn, would seek to form a communication link with the government, so they would have a conduit to the kidnappers through us. But what I did say to Phil was that we should put this on an official basis: that

he undertakes this job as a representative of the union. And if at any time I decide to call you off, I'll call you off.

O'Sullivan was keen to become involved. He was a personal friend of both Garret FitzGerald, the minister for foreign affairs, and Paddy Donegan, the minister for defence, and he felt his contacts might be of use. Flynn was highly thought of within Fianna Fáil, but the Government parties regarded him as a pariah. Later, FitzGerald, as Taoiseach, resigned from the Irish Anti-Apartheid Movement when it refused to ban him and other Sinn Féin representatives from membership. Flynn went home and waited for the phone call, which didn't come until 11.30pm. An envelope containing another taped message had been dropped through the letterbox of the presbytery in Monkstown in south Dublin. O'Sullivan drove him there immediately and they got the tape from Father Thomas Murphy, the parish priest of St Patrick's.

The problem was the message hadn't said which presbytery in Monkstown. There were a few. So Phil and I went around all of them. The priest was very kind. We told him what the score was. He was very civil, considering the time we called at. But we got the tape anyway, and we headed back to the union office in the city and we put it on the machine and listened to it.

The message was long and rambling. Through Herrema's faltering voice could clearly be heard Gallagher's frustration that the threat to Ferenka's future hadn't exerted pressure on the Government, and especially Cooney, to negotiate. The message, recorded that afternoon, said: 'This is a message from the Irish Liberation Organisation, Monday, 13 October 1975. They state that Father O'Mahony is no longer acceptable but that the general secretary (sic) of the local government clerical workers union, Philip Flynn, is acceptable to work with AZKO and the Dutch government in putting pressure on the Irish government to get me released in exchange for these three people – Hyland, Dugdale and Mallon.

'If you ask for proof that I am alive again, they threaten to cut my foot off and send it to you. I call on Ferenka workers to mount a 1,000-strong picket on Leinster House when the Irish government is meeting. It will be more positive than 2,000 demonstrations against my abduction. I do not understand why these three prisoners – one of them is the mother of a young child – cannot be released. Surely the secret police can quite easily get them again, as no special conditions are asked when they are let go. Is an Irish government minister's principles more important than the life of a Dutchman?

'Mentally and physically I have suffered already. Please do not put my life in further danger by looking for me. I have been told that should the secret police find where I am being kept, there will be a fight and they say they will not give the Irish government the satisfaction of getting me back alive, unless the demands are met.

'Please ask the International Red Cross, the Dutch government and AZKO to put further pressure on the Irish government for my release. Please help me. Love to my family. The old codeword was Tornado Sailing Boat. The new codeword will be – and my family will recognise this – Stamp

Collection, Sweden, France, the Netherlands and Ireland.'

Herrema's wife confirmed that the new code was genuine. Her husband had recently begun collecting stamps. The reference to Sweden was because he had an uncle there, to France because he went there on holidays, the Netherlands because he was Dutch and Ireland because that was where he lived. Flynn called the Dutch embassy in the early hours of the morning to tell them about the message, while O'Sullivan phoned Donegan, who called to the union office in person to pick up a typed transcript of the tape.

On Tuesday, October 14, Flynn called a press conference, at which he dutifully repeated Gallagher's message and accused the government of putting a man's life at risk by refusing to talk. He asked rhetorically whether Cosgrave wanted Herrema to be shot as an excuse for introducing more repressive laws aimed at republicans. Gallagher was delighted with Flynn's performance, but the government was furious with him. Cooney publicly attacked him, as did FitzGerald. But behind the public posturing, FitzGerald, at least, understood that he was playing a game and was secretly supportive of what he was doing. When Flynn threatened to pull out early on because of the heat he was getting from the Special Branch, FitzGerald told O'Sullivan to make sure Flynn kept the kidnappers talking.

There was a lot of fervent politicking in the background as O'Sullivan tried to link up a chain of communication between the kidnappers and the government. In Cosgrave's absence, the Tánaiste, Brendan Corish, was in charge of the country, but he refused point-blank to meet him. 'I called Garret and then went over to him in his house in Rathmines, had a cup of tea with him and told him the whole story,' O'Sullivan remembers.

I was very anxious to let the government know what the true situation was, that Phil was not engaged in an adventure of his own making, that he was not on his own and that it was the union that was behind this. Garret understood what was going on and he said, 'I'll try and get someone in touch with you.' And the upshot of all that was that they gave me Garvey (Edmund Garvey, the Garda Commissioner). I was invited into the Department of Justice in Stephen's Green. He had a deputy in the shadows taking notes. It was a farce.

The whole idea was to give me a lecture about Phil Flynn; he had IRA connections and all that kind of thing. I said, 'I'm not aware of his IRA connections. I know he has republican sympathies. I know he's a member of Sinn Féin. But then an awful lot of people are members of Sinn Féin. I have no reason to take any action against him for involvement in politics. It's a free country.' I said, 'I know Phil Flynn better than you do. He's my assistant general secretary. I work with him on a daily basis and I won't listen to bullshit from you.'

Then he told me that they'd checked me out and I was alright, and I thanked him, in an ironic fashion, for his kindness. Then I pointed out to him that I took an oath of allegiance to the Constitution in 1944 when I was commissioned into the army, and it was long before he was around, and I could still ream it off to this day in the Irish language in which I took it, and I didn't have to trade my credentials in front of any goddamn Garda commissioner. He carried on ranting and raving about Flynn and I said very plainly to him, 'If you don't want this communication set up, don't bother your arse. Because I'll tell Flynn to come off it and I'll tell the press that I've told him to come off it and why I've told him to come off it.' So that took Garvey down a peg or two.

But unknown to O'Sullivan, his efforts to establish a third party contact between the kidnappers and the government were a smokescreen. Gallagher and Coyle had already written off any hope of getting Dugdale, Mallon and Hyland out, and their sole interest now was in using Flynn to get as big a ransom as they could out of Ferenka. The company had indicated that they were willing to pay 'a substantial sum' to get Herrema back. Some time after his press conference on Tuesday, Flynn managed to lose his Special Branch detail. He met Gallagher in a house near The Heath, County Laois. Gallagher and Coyle realised now that Flynn was in no position to guarantee them immunity from the IRA and that the wisest move would be for them to leave the country.

Gallagher listed the terms under which they would release Herrema. Ferenka would hand over £2.5m sterling to them. Flynn would deliver the money to Gallagher and Coyle in a suitcase. A pilot, whom Flynn knew, would land a light aircraft on Kilbeggan racecourse in County Wesmeath and fly to a small airstrip in France. From there, another transport would take them and the money to their eventual destination, which, according to Herrema, who discussed the plan with Gallagher, was Tanzania, the socialist republic in East Africa. Flynn would then drive Herrema to Dublin, where AZKO would announce that they were willing to honour the national wage agreement, a curtsy to Gallagher's leftist politics, and guarantee Ferenka's future in Limerick for ten years.

❖❖❖

After his meeting with Garvey, O'Sullivan went to Jury's Hotel in Ballsbridge late on Tuesday night to meet Flynn. He had a ransom note with him. It mentioned the £2.5m and a light aircraft and was written by Coyle, which O'Sullivan took as evidence that she was now in charge of the operation. 'My impression is that at some point she took over,' he says.

> The ransom note, she wrote it and I burnt it. It was on a scrap of paper, handwritten. It was her instructions. She didn't want me to know the content of the note, but I insisted on it. The ransom was two-and-a half million and an aircraft to land at a certain place. Phil called the employers and they came and met us in the hotel and he told them what they were demanding.

O'Sullivan came away from the meeting with the impression that the company was measuring Herrema's worth and it was less than £2.5m. In the end they agreed to hand over the ransom, but not until after Herrema was set free. It could be paid outside the country, it was suggested. Gallagher was furious. Not only would there be no release until they had their money, he told Flynn, but the original plan to go abroad had changed. No one was going to chase him and Coyle out of their own country, he insisted. The new plan was that when the plane landed on the racecourse, a decoy couple – probably PJ and Bridie Bailey – would get into it and fly to France in place of the two kidnappers. The Gardaí and the IRA would presume Gallagher and Coyle had skipped the country, and the heat would be off them.

On Wednesday night Gallagher wrote another statement that reflected his anger and frustration. All week he'd been reading reports about Cosgrave's visit to Rome and also FitzGerald's criticisms of the United States over its relationship with the ailing Spanish dictator Franco, who had recently ordered the execution of five political prisoners. He went to Herrema's room, handed him the new script and asked him to read it several times to familiarise himself with the pronunciation of the words.

The statement read: 'I am being allowed to tape this final message by the Irish Liberation Movement on Thursday, October 18 (sic). I am disappointed to learn that still the Irish cabinet doesn't even consider changing their attitude towards the release of the prisoners, which these people demand in exchange for my life. It is having double standards when Mr FitzGerald criticises America of co-operation with the Spanish government, but then turns around and adopts a Franco-type attitude with the organisation who abducted me. Would their principle remain as now if the life of a government person or a member of the opposition party was in danger?

'I have been told that the bulk of Mallon's sentence was imposed for escaping from jail. Is that fair? Dr Dugdale got nine years for trying to save the lives of young Irishmen who were dying on hunger strike in English prisons. Hyland stated publicly, I am told, at his trial, that he would never use a gun against the Irish police.

'Should Mr Cosgrave and his family live and pray the rest of their lives in Rome, it doesn't absolve them from the moral responsibility to my family and to myself to use their influence to save my life. Also, the churchmen who plead with my abductors should realise that an appeal to the Irish president would be of more use to stop this madness, which prevails on both sides of the affair. You think I criticise men harshly, but what can I do under these circumstances, when people who can help me either turn a deaf ear or leave the country.'

It ended with the codeword, 'Stamp Collection'. The tape was left for collection in a house in Santry in north Dublin.

❖❖❖

On Thursday, October 16, while the government was sitting down to discuss the text of the message, there was panic at the house in Monasterevin. The Gardaí were in the area and were conducting house-to-house searches in St Evin's Park. It was too late for Gallagher and Coyle to attempt to move their hostage from the house. Gallagher burst into Herrema's room at about eleven o'clock in the morning and ordered him to get up. They were going up to the attic. Coyle gathered up all the evidence of their presence in the house and took it up with them. The three sat in tense silence for five hours while they waited for the Gardaí to arrive. Just before four o'clock, they heard the front door open. Herrema was lying on the ground. Gallagher lay on top of him, pushed his gun into the back of his neck and told him not to move. Coyle lay down too. The Gardaí searched the house, but found nothing. Herrema has a vivid recollection of one of them opening the trapdoor:

There were three of us in the attic and I will never know how he didn't see us. I saw the policeman opening the attic. I saw his face but he didn't see us. He had a battery torch. We were lying low on the ground, flat. How he didn't see us is something I can't explain. But maybe it was good that he didn't find us. I had Eddie's gun in the back of my neck. I think he would have shot me had I made a noise.

When the Gardaí left, the three breathed a sight of relief. Coyle suggested leaving Herrema in the attic. They brought a sheet up and told him to make a bed for himself. On the evening news it was reported that Paddy Cooney had issued a response to speculation that he was involved in secret talks with the kidnappers. 'There has been no deal, there is no deal, there will be no deal,' he said. To engage in any kind of dialogue with them would 'literally put in danger any citizen, at any time, that some ruthless people put their eye on as a hostage.' Just before midnight, Gallagher and Coyle seemingly felt sorry for Herrema and took him down from the attic. It had been a long day. The search was a close thing. But their relief wouldn't last long. It was only a temporary reprieve.

On the morning of Saturday, 18 October, the Gardaí picked up Brian McGowan in Tullamore. His alibi for the morning of the kidnapping had been checked and found to be false. He wasn't with John Magee after all. He was arrested under Section 30 of the Offences Against the State Act and taken to Portlaoise. At the back of his house they found the blue Fiat Coupe that Gallagher and Bailey had bought in Newbridge. It was taken away for forensic examination. Gallagher's fingerprints were all over the interior.

McGowan admitted meeting Gallagher and Coyle in Tommy Dolan's pub. He said Gallagher came to him looking for a safe house. But under interrogation he insisted that he had no direct involvement in the kidnapping and didn't know where Herrema was being held.

At 9am on Monday, his forty-eight hour period of detention expired and he was told he was free to go. He asked if he could have a lift back to Tullamore and he was told he could if anyone was going that way. He set off on his own, intending to hitch. Two Gardaí working on the investigation – Detective Inspectors John Courtney and Myles Hawkshaw – pulled over on the road and offered him a lift. McGowan, according to evidence later offered in court, had a change of heart during the journey and decided to confess everything. Just past Mountmellick the detectives pulled into a layby. McGowan was cautioned and he made a statement in which he admitted his full involvement in the kidnapping. He said he didn't know where Herrema was, but the last he knew was that they were taking him to a cottage in Kildangan that he thought was owned by PJ and Bridie Bailey.

❖❖❖

Gallagher was agitated on Sunday. It's likely that he got wind of the arrest and the discovery of the car that linked McGowan to him. He must have wondered would McGowan crack under questioning. He was ready to get out. That night he got a message to Flynn, telling him to come to Monasterevin the following night. The plan was to meet in the priest's house just outside the town, where

Gallagher first persuaded Flynn to become involved. He would bring Herrema, dressed in a blue boiler suit, and deliver him into Flynn's care.

The following morning, Flynn held a press conference at which he maintained the pretence that the release of Dugdale, Mallon and Hyland was still an issue, and complained that Special Branch surveillance was making it impossible for him to operate in any meaningful way. He spent a couple of hours losing them that night, then pointed his car in the direction of Monasterevin.

Herrema says that Gallagher's mood that day was fatalistic. In the afternoon he told him he expected the Gardaí at the door at any minute. PJ Bailey was getting ready to leave his house that night to take Gallagher and the prisoner to Flynn when the Gardai arrived at his home in Canal Harbour. Bridie was there, as were the Halls. The four were arrested under Section 30 of the Offences Against the State Act and taken to Naas. PJ toughed out the questions, but Bridie broke and told them that Gallagher and Coyle had Herrema in her brother's house, 1410 St Evin's Park. When Bailey and Gallagher failed to show up at the rendezvous point, Flynn presumed something had gone wrong. He turned his car around and returned to Dublin. The following morning the the main news bulletin reported that the Gardaí had surrounded a house in Monasterevin.

❖❖❖

Detective Sergeant Patrick Sheil of the Special Branch was the first into the house. By then it was already surrounded by armed Gardaí, backed up by army snipers. At 6.50am on

Tuesday, 21 October, Sheil and three other plainclothes detectives charged up the path to the house, kicked down the door and ran inside with their guns drawn. Gallagher and Coyle were upstairs and ran straight into the box room, where Herrema was sleeping. In the downstairs hall, Detective Sergeant Edward O'Dea said through a loudhailer: 'Gallagher, this is the Gardaí. The house is surrounded by Gardaí and army. Come out with your hands up,' at which point, Gallagher, with a gun in each hand, started shooting indiscriminately. He fired off six shots, hitting doors, walls and window frames upstairs, and screamed, 'Fuck off, you cowardly, dirty cunts. Come up and get me. If you come up the stairs, I'll blow your fucking heads off. I'll blow the head off this fucking Dutchman.' Herrema's voice could be faintly heard, imploring, 'Please stay away. Don't come into the house. He has a gun to my head. He'll shoot me.'

The exchanges continued for half an hour, O'Dea calling on Gallagher and Coyle to surrender and Gallagher shouting obscenities back. He threw a lemonade bottle at the window, showering glass on to Gardaí in the front garden. He ordered Herrema to tell the Gardaí that he'd been wired with explosives, although he hadn't. When Gallagher spent the afternoon reiterating the original demand for the release of the three IRA prisoners, the Gardaí accepted that it was a siege situation. Gallagher and Coyle barricaded themselves and their prisoner into the box room, using two mattresses, while the Gardaí dug in directly beneath them in the living room and prepared themselves for a protracted standoff.

With no previous experience of siege situations, Garvey, the Garda Commissioner, asked for the advice of the

Metropolitan Police in London, who four weeks earlier brought a successful end to the so-called Spaghetti House Siege in Knightsbridge. Three gunmen had forced their way into an Italian restaurant, with the intention of stealing the week's takings. Nine members of staff were held at gunpoint in the basement after the alarm was raised and police officers surrounded the building. The police were commended for their patience in wearing down and demoralising the gunmen during the six-day siege. Garvey was advised to take a softly-softly approach and to break the will of the kidnappers slowly, though few would have forecast the impasse lasting three times longer than the Knightsbridge standoff.

The six terraced houses in St Evin's Park were evacuated while Gardaí kept submachine guns permanently trained on the upstairs window of 1410. The armoured cars and jeeps driven by helmeted soldiers with semi-automatic weapons lent the quiet, nondescript housing estate the air of a war zone. An ambulance waited on standby with supplies of Herrema's blood type, along with a coronary care unit, in case the worst happened.

Gallagher fortified the barricade in the bedroom, using a heavy steel bedstead and a chair. He taped a blanket and a bedspread over the front window to stop Gardaí seeing into the room and removed the glass laths from the louvred window above the door so he and Coyle could hear what was happening downstairs. That night, the three lay side by side on the floor, sharing the warmth of one another's bodies in the bitter crosswind produced by the broken window and the gap above the door.

Part of the Garda strategy was to keep the kidnappers on the edge of hunger and exhaustion. Arc lights were used to light up the front of the house and deprive them of sleep, while the food rations – one ham sandwich and a glass of milk in the morning and half that in the evening – were enough to stop them from starving, but not to satisfy them.

On Wednesday afternoon, the second day of the siege, two officers from Scotland Yard arrived on an RAF Nimrod jet with a sophisticated piece of listening equipment capable of picking up a conversation from five hundred yards away. A psychologist was brought in to eavesdrop on the conversations and to advise the Gardaí of any dramatic changes in the mood of the kidnappers. However, Gallagher and Coyle suspected they were being listened to and resorted to communicating in whispers. Sensitive microphones were then placed in the ceiling of the hall underneath them, but they could pick up little through the thick underlay of the carpet.

At dawn on Thursday, Gallagher demanded to see Chief Superintendent Larry Wren, well known to all IRA men as the Garda in charge of national security and intelligence. Wren arrived at 9am. Gallagher wanted to cut a deal, but he wasn't prepared to talk without seeing the whites of Wren's eyes. He wanted him upstairs in the box room, but Wren refused, for fear of being taken hostage himself.

On Friday, Coyle wrote her name and the date on the wallpaper – 24 October, 1975 – suggesting that they may have considered surrendering that day. The conditions in which they were living were appalling. According to Herrema, they tried drinking their own urine because they had no water. For the first few days they urinated into a milk bottle and defecated onto pieces of newspaper. They were supplied with a potty, which Herrema emptied out the window at the start of every new day and some luckless Gardaí took turns to scrub the path with a brush and disinfectant. At 11am Herrema appeared at the window, the first public sighting of him for exactly three weeks. Looking thin and jaundiced, he drew back the red and white, leaf-patterned curtains and, through the broken window, called to watching newsmen: 'Help me ... Tell the police to stay away ... Please save my life ... Tell them not to come near ... Help me ...' Gallagher had a gun pressed to the back of his neck.

The decision was then made to move the press away from the front of the house. It was claimed that Gallagher and Coyle had a transistor radio in the room and knew too much of what was happening outside from listening to the news. The real reason was the fear that the daily sight of Herrema pleading for his life on television would put pressure on the government's hardline stand on negotiating.

❖❖❖

At the start of the second week of the siege, the Gardaí removed slates from the roof of 1410 to gain access to the attic, heightening speculation that they were planning to storm the house. Detective Inspector John Murphy of Kevin Street Station retrieved an overcoat and a newspaper that Gallagher and Coyle had left behind when they fled to the attic on the day of the previous Garda search. Gallagher heard the noise above him and fired a shot through the ceiling. It took Gardaí several hours to get him calm again.

The siege wore on into its second week, with little now to

demarcate one day from the one that went before. Herrema composed his own crossword on the inside lid of a chess box and sang Dutch songs. Gallagher continued shouting abuse at the Gardaí and forced Herrema to the window at regular intervals to demand the release of the three prisoners. Soon the story dropped down the news lists. By the beginning of the second week, some senior Gardaí, worried about the mental stability of Gallagher and Coyle as the siege dragged on, were giving serious consideration to the idea of bringing it to an end. Two plans were considered. One involved pumping an odourless gas into the box room to knock out the three occupants. The gas was tested on soldiers in the Curragh, but they reported that they were aware of its effects before they were rendered unconscious, and the plan was scratched. The other idea was to fix small quantities of explosives to the ceiling and bring the floor of the box room down. In the end it was regarded as being too dangerous.

Paddy Cooney urged patience. Wren was talking to Gallagher, developing a relationship with him. The kidnappers were given fresh clothes and underwear in an attempt to win their trust. By Wednesday, 30 October, they were ready to discuss terms for their surrender. Gallagher had asked for legal counsel, and that night, Seamus Sorohan, the well-known barrister, arrived at the house, having earlier appealed for an urgent adjournment in a case in which he was involved. A solicitor, Stanley Siev, also showed up. Garvey was rushed through the cordons to the house in a car with its light flashing. Gallagher and Coyle wanted advice on their prospects at a trial if they gave up now.

The siege might well have ended that weekend had

Gardaí not tried to tighten the screw by gaining a foothold on the upstairs of the house. It was reported that some senior officers were in favour of taking it over by force. On Friday, 1 November, it was decided to remove a pane of opaque glass from the upstairs bathroom to give the Gardaí control of the landing. Detective Sergeant Michael Egan was at the top of a ladder, chipping away at the putty around the window, when he heard a loud bang. Suddenly, his hand was covered in blood. Gallagher had heard a noise at the window and gone out to the landing to investigate. He saw Egan's hand moving up and down the outside frame and fired a shot from his .38. The bullet shattered Egan's index finger, which subsequently had to be amputated in Laois County Hospital.

This incident undid all the work that Wren had done to build up trust with the kidnappers. Gallagher ranted and raved about being double-crossed. The Gardaí were so worried about his mental stability that weekend that they used sandbags and lengths of timber to block the bottom of the stairs for fear that he'd burst out of the room and come down the stairs shooting. He refused to speak to Wren, sending Herrema to the window with messages. Gardaí below held up large signs with questions written on them, to try to find out the lie of the land: were there any explosives in the room, were his feet tied, how many guns did Gallagher and Coyle have? Herrema answered with barely perceptible hand and facial gestures. They couldn't make out whether he said there were two or three guns in the room.

It was Tuesday before Gallagher and Wren had another

reasoned discussion. By that point the Gardaí knew that the siege had just a matter of hours to run. Gallagher was cracking up. The listening devices had picked up the sound of him groaning and complaining of a stiff neck and headaches. Gallagher was convinced he had meningitis, but doctors later confirmed what Herrema suspected, that his illness was psychosomatic. Emotions such as stress and anxiety will sometimes manifest themselves in bogus physical symptoms. According to Herrema:

> He had these cramps in his neck that he was complaining about for a couple of days. He was really in a bad situation at the end. He really didn't know what he had, but he thought that it might be meningitis. He was crying, just weeping all the time. I had seen this kind of thing before when I was in a prisoner camp. I knew it was psychosomatic. Of course I did not tell him this.

On Wednesday, 6 November, there were talks between Gallagher and Coyle and Garvey and Wren. These discussions were the subject of controversy during the eventual trial and remain a source of bitterness for Herrema today. A deal was struck in the house relating to how much time Gallagher and Coyle would serve in prison if they gave themselves up, though its details have never been made public. Herrema can't remember the precise prison time specified, but believes it may have been four years. Garvey visited the house three times during the day and left in the evening with Wren to go to see Cooney. The terms of the deal, which was ratified by the Cabinet, were written on a piece of paper and witnessed by Herrema, who was asked by Gallagher to hold onto it for safekeeping. He put it in his inside pocket.

At 8pm the following night, seventeen days after the siege began, thirty-five days since they snatched Herrema on his way to work, Coyle asked for medication, claiming that Herrema had cramps in his neck. But Gallagher had been heard moaning, 'Christ, I'm dying,' and Coyle was told they could have all the medical care they needed if they came down the stairs. Three-quarters of an hour later, she asked for a doctor to be sent to the room, but the request was refused. At 9.05pm she told Wren that they were coming downstairs. A microphone at the foot of the stairs recorded their surrender.

Wren: Okay, well now, before you come down, throw your guns out the window.

Coyle: Take the armed men out of the house then.

Wren: Oh no, not till you throw out … You've got to throw out your guns and I'll have to take away the barricades then. Throw your guns out first. You've nothing to fear. There's nobody going to interfere with you. And I'm going to stay here to ensure that … There's no danger of it happening, in any case.

Upstairs, Gallagher was lying on one of the mattresses, holding his cramped neck. Coyle sat on the floor with her back against the door. Herrema stood in the middle of the room. His kidnappers handed him their guns and he brought them to the window.

Herrema: Throwing the guns down now.

Wren: Okay, right.

The .32 pistol hit the ground.

Wren: Fair enough. Okay, there's one down. Okay.

Herrema: I'm going to throw the second one out.

Wren: Okay.

The second .32 hit the ground. Wren gambled on the fact that there were three guns in the room.

Wren: Right, third one.

Coyle: Take the men out of the house now.

Wren: Throw the third one out. You have a third one.

There was a lengthy pause before Gallagher handed his beloved long-barrelled Smith and Wesson revolver to Herrema. 'Come on, Eddie, give me the gun,' Herrema told him. 'Come on, let me have it.' It was dropped out of the window and – in a neat piece of symbolism – it broke when it hit the ground. Before they left the room, Gallagher gave Herrema a live round from one of the .38s as a souvenir. The bedroom door was opened and they stepped out onto the landing.

Wren: Now, let me get a chance here of removing some of these barricades. Take your time for a minute or two now because I've got barricades here I want to remove ... Take your time now. Take your time.

Coyle came down the stairs first, followed by Herrema, then Gallagher. Coyle had an overcoat draped over her arm, while Gallagher, heavily bearded after almost three weeks in the house, had his hands sunk in his pockets.

Detective: Come on, you're all right. Come on, Marion.

Wren: Take your time. It's all right ... Drop your coat, Marion.

Coyle: There's nothing in it.

Wren: You've nothing in it?

Coyle: Not a thing.

She took the coat off her arm and put it on.

Wren: One by one now, please ... Okay ... Take those out of her way there ...

Detective: Eddie, take your hands out of your pockets, please ... Okay.

Wren: One by one. Take your time. Take your time. One by one. Come on, Doctor. Okay, mind yourself.

Detective: Come on, Eddie, easy now. Put your hands on your head, would you? That's the boy.

❖❖❖

Bearded, but looking fit and well, Tiede Herrema walked from the house unaided. Gallagher and Coyle were taken into the kitchen and arrested. They weren't handcuffed, and they were taken out to separate Garda cars and driven to the Bridewell in Dublin. In a follow up search at the house in Monasterevin, Gardaí discovered a book wrapped in clothing and hidden behind the cylinder in the hot press. It was Eddie Gallagher's copy of *Who's Who in Ireland*.

Dr Herrema was driven to the Dutch ambassador's house in Dundrum in south Dublin to be reunited with his wife, Elisabeth, who was flying back from Holland on an AZKO private jet. But the ambassador had gone to the Curragh, having been told that Herrema was being taken to the military hospital for a medical check-up. Garret FitzGerald and his wife Joan also showed up, to discover that no one was home. A neighbour took Herrema and the FitzGeralds in.

He was in the living room, drinking tea and telling the FitzGeralds about his long ordeal when he was told that there was someone at the door to see him. 'It was Wren,' he recalls.

He was standing at the front door and he said to me, 'You'd better give me that document, because you're heading off to Holland.' I said to him that I promised Eddie Gallagher that it would not get into the wrong hands. He said, 'We are the Gardaí. How could that be the wrong hands?' So I gave it him, and I regret very much that I did that now. Because the next thing I heard about the agreement was when Wren was on the news the next day denying that it ever existed. That made me very angry, because I trusted him. He let me down.

The Gardaí did deny that a deal was made in return for the surrender, as did the Government in the days after the siege. Paddy Cooney was emphatic on the point. 'If you mean was there any concession made to the kidnappers – none at all,' he told reporters. 'None at all?' he was asked. 'None at all,' he replied. But a deal *was* done, though it is unlikely that the contract that Herrema had in his pocket had any real basis in law, since it was signed under duress, with one party holding a gun. Still, Herrema remains upset about the episode:

When you give your word, you give your word. I gave Eddie Gallagher my word, and I let him down. I gave the agreement to Mr Wren. I trusted him. He was there in the house all the time in Monasterevin. He was my contact man. I liked him. He was very relaxed and friendly. I thought I was putting it in safe hands by giving it to him, but I was wrong about that. What we agreed in that house should have stood. Of course, people will say I'm mad to say this, because you cannot make a legal agreement with someone if they are pointing a gun at you. But that is not the way I feel. I gave Eddie Gallagher and Marion Coyle my word, and my word is very, very important to me. You must understand that we had this relationship while we were together that was based on trust. Very early on in the kidnapping, Eddie Gallagher told me that there was no way he was going to shoot me unless I tried to escape. I made a promise to him that I would not try to escape, and he made a promise to me that I would not be killed. That was the understanding. We trusted each other. But this one time I couldn't keep my word, and that is something I have regretted for thirty years.

❖❖❖

In the aftermath of the kidnapping it was clear that a fondness had developed between Herrema and Gallagher. Asked whether he hated his captors for the ordeal they put him through, Herrema said, 'I have children of the same age, and I see them (Gallagher and Coyle) as children with a lot of problems. I must say, that if they were my children, I would do my utmost to help them.' At their trial in February 1976, Gallagher and Coyle stood down their legal team and conducted their own defence. Gallagher called Herrema to the witness stand, but refused to subject him to a rigorous cross-examination, as a senior counsel would have. The two even shared jokes across the floor of the courtroom.

During the course of trial, Gallagher railed against what he said was a campaign of character assassination waged against him by senior members of the republican movement. He angrily denied the claim, planted in the press, that he had carried out robberies for his own personal benefit.

The Herrema kidnapping, he said, was part of a just war, one in which he and Coyle had often risked their lives to rid the country of the shame of occupation by a foreign force.

Then he spoke about Frank Stagg, the young IRA Volunteer who had just died while on hunger strike at Wakefield Prison in England. Stagg had ended his first fast at the same time as the London bomb team in June 1974. But while the Price sisters, Feeney and Kelly were all moved back to Northern Ireland within a year, Stagg's application for a transfer was turned down. He began refusing food again, and this time carried the protest through to the end. His last wish was to be buried in his home town in Mayo, with full military honours, his coffin driven along the same route as Michael Gaughan's had been, from Dublin to Ballina. Gaughan's funeral had been turned into a paramilitary show of strength by the Provisionals, and Cosgrave had taken it as an affront to the authority of the State. The plane that was to bring Stagg's body to Dublin was diverted by the government to Shannon. After scuffles at the airport, the coffin was taken to Ballina, where it was buried, not in the republican plot, but in another grave dug by Gardaí, then entombed under eighteen inches of concrete and guarded round-the-clock. Six months later, when the furore died down, the IRA tunnelled under the concrete, exhumed the body and, with a priest present, reburied it in the republican plot. Gallagher said that there had been a lot of sympathy for the 'anguish of Mrs Herrema' but 'hardly a murmur' for the family of Stagg, whose body had been abducted in broad daylight, and 'to this day, the Free State sit like ghouls on top of his grave, in defiance of his family and his last wishes.'

He mentioned the deal that he and Coyle had cut with Garvey, the Garda Commissioner, whom he called as a witness. He attempted to cross-examine him on the document, but became frustrated when his method of questioning was ruled out of order. He gave up, describing the trial as a fit-up. He thanked 'those people around the country who opened their doors to us during the past few years,' and added, 'Hopefully we will be back with them again before very long.' Coyle told the court that Gallagher was one of the bravest and most honourable soldiers she had ever worked with. She said that Paddy Cooney should have been in the dock instead of them, charged with criminally mismanaging his department. 'I make no apologies for my actions,' she added.

Gallagher was sentenced to twenty years in prison and Coyle to fifteen. McGowan and Walsh each received eight years for their part in the kidnapping, while David Dunne was given a three-year suspended sentence. At a separate trial, Michael Hall and PJ Bailey were jailed for five years each. Gallagher and Coyle remained defiant until the end. Gardaí had to clear the court as the two shouted threats at the president of the Special Criminal Court, Justice Pringle, referring to an incendiary device that had apparently been sent to him in the post. As she was led from the dock, Coyle shouted, 'Hey, Pringle, the letter bomb is a warning you did not heed,' while Gallagher added, 'It'll not be a letter bomb you'll get next time. You have been sentenced, Pringle.'

But for Eddie Gallagher and Marion Coyle, the war was over.

CHAPTER FOUR

Prisoner in Bandit Country
The Kidnapping of Ben Dunne

'What would Kojak do in this situation?'
Father Dermod McCarthy

Friday, 17 October 1981. Ben Dunne thought he'd been lucky. Just beyond the border crossing at Killeen, County Louth, on the main Dublin to Belfast road, a green Opel Ascona travelling in the opposite direction had swerved into his lane and he had to wrestle his black Mercedes into the hard shoulder to avoid a head-on collision. He hit the brakes so hard that when he looked in his rear view mirror he could see plumes of black smoke rising from his tyres. The other car, which had also pulled into the hard shoulder, began reversing back towards him. Dunne was getting ready to joke with the other driver about how they'd cheated death, when four masked men, one of them carrying a rifle, sprang from the car, pulled open his door and dragged him out onto the road. In a daze, he was pushed into the back of the Ascona, where a hood was pulled over his head. He asked, 'Are you going to shoot me?' One of the gang said, 'Keep your head down. Don't ask questions and you won't be shot.'

They drove for about twenty miles. Then, with a member of the gang holding either arm, Dunne was taken out of the car and marched into what he presumed, from the foul smell and the mud beneath his feet, was some kind of pigsty. He was asked for the phone numbers of his wife and his father, which is when he realised he was being kidnapped for ransom. 'What do you think you're worth?' one of the men asked him. Dunne replied, 'Nothing. You'll get nothing for me.' His hands were tied and he was left sitting on a crate for a couple of hours.

Soon they were on the move again. The security forces had by now been alerted about what had happened, and the gang was using a field radio to monitor police and army movements in the area. Dunne heard several references to the 'Brits' being 'too close'. They took him, again with a member of the gang holding him under the arm, and ran with him across a number of fields. Dunne, who was overweight, became short of breath and asked them to take it easy. They stopped and he was pushed into a ditch, where he was made to lie on his side for another two hours. When they were satisfied that the area was safe, they started moving again, walking in what appeared to Dunne to be the lee of a hedge, close to a road. Whenever he heard a car pass, a gun was pressed into his neck or his ribs and he was told to keep his head down. Eventually they pushed him out onto the road, where he was bundled into the back seat of another car. After a half-hour drive, he was taken into the farmhouse in South Armagh that would be his prison for the next six days and nights.

Dunne had been on his way to Portadown, County

Armagh, for the opening of a new outlet. He was almost certainly followed from the time he left his home in Castleknock, County Dublin at 8.30am that Friday morning and it's likely that two vehicles were involved: a blue Ford Transit van and a motorcycle. The van, like the Ascona, had been hijacked two nights earlier on a notorious stretch of the Concession Road in South Armagh, where the local IRA acquired most of the vehicles for their operations.

A ransom demand of £500,000 was phoned to the head office of Dunnes Stores that morning. Ben's wife, Mary, who had been out shopping, was told of her husband's abduction on returning home by a neighbour who had heard about it on the radio.

In the house in South Armagh, Dunne was left lying on a hard floor, with a pillow propping up his hooded head. At meal times, the material was pulled up as far as the top of his mouth to allow him to eat. Apart from that, he spent the next week in a state of almost total sensory deprivation. He was warned that if he attempted to remove his hood they would shoot him in the head. 'They were rough characters,' he remembered later. 'You knew they meant business.'

❖❖❖

Nowhere in Ireland was the allegiance to the IRA and the armed struggle stronger than in South Armagh, and no other posting anywhere in the world carried with it a greater threat of death for members of the British army. The mere mention of the name is enough to strike terror into the heart of any soldier who survived a tour of duty there. The 123 troops and forty-two RUC officers killed there since

1971 account for one fifth of all military casualties during the Troubles. Its area of less than two hundred square miles is defined to the south and west by the border with the Republic, to the east by the main Dublin to Belfast road and to the north by an invisible line running from Mountmorris to Keady. At the height of the Troubles, the magnificent centrepiece of Slieve Gullion was salted with watchtowers, where the security forces kept tabs on the 23,000 people – almost all of them Catholic – who called it home. Its topography made South Armagh the ideal theatre for guerrilla warfare. Death lurked behind every bramble bush and rock wall. Bales of hay could conceal snipers. Milk churns could be packed with explosives.

It wasn't just the countryside and the proximity to the border that gave the IRA the advantage in South Armagh. They operated with either the active support or the acquiescence of the local population. With people too frightened, or in most cases simply unwilling, to assist the security services, it became an impossible theatre of operations for them.

Hostility and suspicion had been part of the natural order in South Armagh long before the observation towers were erected. The area saw some of the bloodiest fighting of the War of Independence but, after partition, found itself, despite its Catholic majority, in the nascent Northern state, a betrayal that helped breed in local people an instinctive distrust of outsiders and a fearsome independence. In 1975, when Merlyn Rees, the secretary of state for Northern Ireland, called the area 'Bandit Country', most locals took it as a backhanded compliment for their refusal to be subjugated. But they preferred to call it 'God's Country'.

As much as they hated the border, the local IRA were adept at using it. In snatching Dunne in the Republic and holding him in the North, they were taking advantage of a problem that has existed since the island was partitioned – the difficulty of coordinating a security response in two jurisdictions. The search for Dunne presented enormous difficulties for the Gardaí and the RUC, not least of which was the lattice of boreens and unapproved roads that criss-crossed the border and offered IRA Volunteers safe passage into and out of the North. In fact, it was often difficult to tell where the Gardaí's jurisdiction ended and the RUC's began. The notional border bisected parishes, roads, even farmers' fields. Sometimes only the colour of the post boxes gave an indication of what side of the border you were on.

At the time, the IRA to all intents and purposes controlled South Armagh. The security forces had virtually abandoned the roads for fear of mines. Almost all military and police movement in the area was by helicopter, with even the refuse from the army bases being choppered out. South Armagh was thought to be so ungovernable that Harold Wilson and Margaret Thatcher both considered offering to redraw the border to place it inside the Republic. But, as Wilson pointed out, it was such a nightmare from a security point of view that he doubted the Irish government would have taken it off their hands. Neither could the sweep of a cartographer's pen change the defiant nature of the people of South Armagh. To them the latest Troubles were part of the same centuries-old war to rid Ireland of British occupation.

Within the IRA, the South Armagh Brigade – or the

Wellington Boot Brigade, as they were nicknamed in Belfast because of their rural background – enjoyed a degree of independence under the command of Tom 'Slab' Murphy, the future chief of staff. In 1981, at the time of the Dunne kidnap, the IRA in South Armagh was planning to import a cache of Redeye surface-to-air missiles, with the intention of shooting a British army helicopter out of the sky. Murphy is said to have taken his inspiration from the mujahadin's success against the Soviets in Afghanistan. By making it unsafe for troops to travel by air, the IRA could score its first real military victory since partition by forcing the British out of South Armagh altogether. Gerry McGeough, a gunrunner from County Tyrone, was eventually sent to the United States, where he made contact with what he thought was an illegal arms dealer, who promised to sell him five missiles for $50,000 each. When he arrived at a warehouse in New Orleans to inspect the merchandise, McGeough discovered he'd been ensnared in an FBI trap and he fled.

The ransom demanded for Dunne may have been intended to finance shipments of Redeyes, though republican sources suggested at the time that the kidnapping wasn't an official operation but the work of a rogue IRA unit known as the Edentubber Group.

Supermarket executives were an attractive target to kidnappers because their employers had instant access to large amounts of used, and therefore untraceable, banknotes. Millions of pounds were passing through the tills of the company's fifty stores every week. Dunnes Stores had grown to become the seventh largest business in Ireland and had begun to extend its fingers into the North. Its flagship store was in the Abbeycentre in north Belfast. Another was opened on North Street in the city. By 1981 there were also outlets in Lisburn, Larne, Antrim, Bangor, Warrenpoint, Newry and Coleraine. The Provisionals may have also figured that, with a business with an annual turnover of close to £15m in the North, Dunne's father would settle quickly to avoid further trouble from them.

Ben Dunne senior was now in his seventies and was preparing to hand over the running of the business to his children, the most colourful of whom was Ben junior. At thirty-four, he was already a joint managing director of Dunnes Stores and also the real energy behind the company. He was a family man and was married to Mary Godwin, a former Aer Lingus air hostess, who had just given birth to their fourth child. Like his father, he liked to be considered a no-frills operator. He never spoke to the press, he never had a minder and, as on the day he travelled to Portadown to inspect the newest outpost in the Dunnes empire, he did all his own driving.

❖❖❖

Many of the faces that were around the Cabinet table during the Herrema kidnapping in 1975 were back again six years later. Garret FitzGerald was now Taoiseach and his line on hostage-taking was even harder than Cosgrave's had been. In 1974, when Lord and Lady Donoughmore were abducted, the Hely-Hutchinson family were told by the Gardaí to have money ready in the event of a ransom demand. The following year, AZKO offered publicly to pay for the safe return of Herrema, without any censure from the authorities about putting guns in the hands of paramilitaries. The Dunne case differed from others in that Garda resources were divided between searching for the missing supermarket executive and thwarting the efforts of his family and friends to pay the kidnappers. The payment of ransom wasn't a crime in itself, but Jim Mitchell, the minister for justice, was told by the attorney general, Peter Sutherland, that it was perfectly acceptable for the Gardaí to confiscate the money. The Garda Commissioner, Patrick McLaughlin, instructed Gardaí to intervene in any attempt to pay the ransom. Mitchell said later that he knew he was putting a man's life on the line, and he said he prayed several times a day that he was doing the right thing.

The political climate was even more hostile to the Provisionals than it was in 1974 or 1975. A backlash of violence was expected in the wake of the recent Maze Prison hunger strike, in which ten Republican prisoners died in protest at the withdrawal of their special category status. It was known that both the IRA and the INLA were on major fundraising drives. Republican paramilitaries were blamed for the growing incidence of local, low profile kidnappings in the Republic and the North. The INLA were involved in the recent kidnappings of AIB branch manager Tom Scully and his family from their home in Rathfarnham, County Dublin, and Anne Hudson, the personal secretary to hotelier Bertram Allen, in Courtown, County Wexford. In the Scully case, the Gardaí staked out the drop for the ransom, but a member of the gang escaped with £30,000 on a motorcyle down a laneway too narrow for a Garda car to follow, while the efforts to extort money from the Allen family continued for almost a year after Hudson was freed in a house in Glenageary in south Dublin. For the Government, kidnappings were becoming worryingly commonplace. FitzGerald remembers:

> Quite apart from the political situation at the time, it was agreed that this kind of crime could not be seen to pay and that was the reason we took the tough line we did in the Dunne case. It wasn't an easy decision to make and it didn't come without a lot of agonising on our parts. A man's life was at stake and it's very difficult to tell a man's wife and his family that you're going to stop them from doing what they need to in order to save his life. But we also had a responsibility to take into account the likely consequences of allowing that amount of money to fall into the hands of subversives, and how many people could be killed in the long term as a result of that money being spent on arms. We felt, as well, that if it were seen to be successful then it would open the floodgates.

The Gardaí forced Dunnes Stores branches throughout the country to lodge their day's takings in the bank each evening, making it difficult for the family to pay the money without making large cash withdrawals that would alert the Special Branch. The effort to save his life became a three-way battle of wits between the Gardaí, the IRA and Dunne's family and friends, who let it be known from the beginning that they were willing to meet the demands. Ben Dunne senior took the news of his son's kidnapping badly, and immediately delegated his friend and financial advisor, Noel Fox, to do whatever was necessary to secure his release. On Friday afternoon, as the Government pleaded with the family not to trade with the kidnappers, Fox met with Dunne's accountant, Oliver Freaney, and Ben junior's friend, Father Dermod McCarthy, in Freaney's office in Dublin to devise a way of getting the money to the kidnappers behind the backs of the Gardaí. According to McCarthy:

> It was a them-and-us situation. We knew the Government had their agenda, but we had our agenda too. And we wanted Ben released. And if that meant paying some money or somebody paying some money somewhere at some stage for Ben, then so be it. But the Government, we knew, were dead against it. I had a conversation with Garret FitzGerald and Jim Mitchell in the Taoiseach's office and I knew where they were coming from. But they knew where we were coming from. We had these meetings in the accountants' offices on St Mary's Road. There was Noel Fox, Oliver Freaney, myself, and a couple of others, and the discussion was how to progress this thing.

McCarthy was a well-known producer and presenter of the popular RTÉ religious affairs programme 'Radharc' and had been a friend of Dunnes for eight or nine years. He performed Ben's marriage to Mary and baptised their children.

> We met at a family get-together. It was the baptism of one of his sister Elizabeth's children. I was based in Athy at the time. This was the early 1970s. I knew a lady in Athy whose brother, Brian McMahon, had been in school with me and was now married to Elizabeth Dunne. I was invited to Elizabeth's house for the baptism. Young Ben was there, or Benny as we used to call him at the time. And he was with this lovely girl from Kilkenny, an air hostess, called Mary Godwin. We got on very well. There was a bit of banter like you'd find at any party. I happened to say to Ben and Mary that I did

special rates for weddings, totally innocently, joking really. To my amazement Ben said, 'We might take you up on that'. After that we met quite a lot socially. As a couple they were really good fun. Ben was the youngest of the family. He was – and still is – brash and outgoing too, maybe a bit over-confident, as young men are, it's par for the course. In the end I did their wedding. And we've stayed in touch ever since. I became a regular visitor to their home. And whenever there was a bit of a problem, I'd be asked for advice or support.

All of Dunne's friends suspected that their phone lines were tapped, and wherever they went they presumed they were being watched. They used all manner of means to lose their Special Branch tails. McCarthy remembers entering hotels through the front door and leaving through a back entrance, and he even spent some time hidden in car boots.

On Saturday morning, 18 October, Fox left Freaney's office and drove to the Fairways Hotel, two miles outside Dundalk on the Dublin to Belfast road. On Friday, a large sum of money had been withdrawn from one of the bank accounts the Gardaí were monitoring. Two detectives followed Fox to the hotel, where he made and received a number of phone calls and, it is believed, was told the rendezvous point for the handover of the money, somewhere in South Armagh. The Gardaí planned to follow him the six miles to the border, where the RUC would take over the surveillance and ambush the gang as they came to collect the money. But the RUC said they would do it only if the handover was done in daylight. Snipers and landmines had made South Armagh a no-go area for the security forces after dark. Knowing this, the gang waited until nightfall to tell Fox to proceed to the rendezvous point. The Gardaí had no choice but to move in on him as he was leaving the hotel, carrying what they described as a substantial amount of money. He was escorted back to Dublin. The gang heard about Fox's interception on the radio news. Dunne heard it at the same time and knew at that point that his life now depended on the resourcefulness of his friends. 'That is when I resigned myself to the fact that the Gardaí have got to do a job,' he said later, 'and if these people are going to shoot me, they are going to shoot me. '

Mary Dunne issued a statement that night telling the IRA that the family had done everything it could to fulfil their demands, but were prevented from doing so. 'We at no time contacted the Gardaí or advised them of what was happening,' she said. 'We will cooperate fully to secure Bernard's release.'

Fox later claimed he had only ever been a decoy. 'Whether Noel was going to hand the money over himself or ask someone else to do it I never found out,' says McCarthy.

> I only have my version of what happened. Other things were going on behind the scenes that I wasn't party to. All I know is that an attempt was made to pay the money on the Saturday night, but the Gardai intercepted it. Subsequently I learned from Ben that the kidnappers were furious when this happened because they knew the Gardaí were following whoever was paying over the money. So they said to him, 'Name somebody whom you can trust and we can trust to progress this thing.' And he named me.

Now Ben didn't know where I was at the time. I was working with 'Radharc' and my work involved quite a bit of travel. I could have been in South America, Africa, Asia, anywhere. I was out of the country maybe three months of each year if you totalled up all the weeks. But, as it happened, I was here. On Sunday morning, I got a call from Father Tom Fehily, who was the parish priest of Porterstown parish, where Ben lived in Castleknock. He said some people had phoned and they wanted to talk to me and could I come out to the house there and take a call. Obviously, they guessed that my phone was tapped. So I went to Fr Fehily's house and the call came.

A Northern voice told me to be in the village of Louth – which I didn't know existed until that point – at four o'clock that afternoon, and not to be followed. He said to go to the telephone kiosk in the village and I'd get another call there. The Gardaí knew what kind of car I drove, so I didn't bring my own car. I drove another one belonging to a brother-in-law of Mary's. As I was driving north I said to myself, 'McCarthy, you're out of your mind. God knows what you're walking yourself into here.' But when you're in my job as a priest, or if you're any kind of friend, then you do things at times which … Let's just say there was no time to rationalise about personal risk.

I arrived in the village of Louth, parked on the street opposite the phone kiosk and I was there about fifteen minutes. There were some kids playing around the kiosk, and that really bothered me. They were in and out of it, playing games, slamming the door. Then they were picking the phone up and making imaginary calls, and I was thinking, 'What if the kidnappers call and the phone is engaged?' Then in my mirror I saw, coming behind me, a guy on a motorbike. He came down quickly through the village, passed me by, a big black helmet on him. I saw the head turning and looking at me, and he went past and I knew straight away that he was checking to see if I was there, and alone. He went on up, did a turn at the church, which was at the end of the village, and then came back down. He had another good look in at me and then drove on again. Eventually the kids moved on. I went to the kiosk and the call came and I was told to go to another kiosk in a village three miles farther north, called Knockbridge. I was told to be there in fifteen minutes.

So I drove to Knockbridge, found the kiosk and I waited. The call came. A Northern accent. A clipped Northern accent, the same voice as had spoken to me in Dublin and in Louth. Very precise. No small talk whatever. The voice said, 'Turn around and reach up over the door. You'll find a piece of paper. Read it and do what it says.' Then down went the phone. So I reached up over the door and there was a piece of paper, about A5 size, and written on it, all in capitals to disguise the handwriting, was an instruction to go back to the middle of Knockbridge and turn right, which would mean heading west. It read: go through three or four crossroads and straight, straight, straight until you come to a junction and then turn left. Proceed along that route until you come to another telephone kiosk on the right hand side of the road.

I did as I was bid, but there was no telephone kiosk. The instructions were designed to get me on that narrow country road and to a certain point where two masked men hopped out in front of me with guns and ordered me to stop. A third man was on the other side of the road, opening the gate into this disused farmyard. I was ushered in and ordered to hide the car, which I did, in a copse of trees off to the left hand side. I remember, as I was hiding the car, realising that I wasn't sure whether I was north or south of the border.

I hid the car and I got out and they searched me. I was wearing a leatherette coat and all I had in my pocket was an apple. I didn't know whether I was going have time to eat, and I knew I was going to be travelling all day, so I just brought an apple to eat later on. They brought me down behind a hayshed. They were quite polite. One of them was doing the talking. He was the second-in-command. The guy who was in charge hardly spoke at all except to give the other man orders. The third man, I remember, had a big field radio with him. We all got down on our hunkers to talk behind this shed, but they were worried that we were too close to the road, so they decided we needed to move. We got up and they marched me along a weed-covered laneway, a track really, which eventually came to a stream. We had to cross the stream, and they were apologising to me about my feet getting wet, which was the least of my worries. So we went along another track and came to a group of disused farmhouses. One of them was a shed with a caked earth floor on which there had been hens or pigs. So we went in there and that's where the conversation took place.

Despite Garda suspicions that McCarthy was the bagman for the ransom payment, he insists that he had no money with him when he met the kidnappers in the shed in Castleroche, a small townland a hundred and fifty yards south of the border in County Louth. The meeting, he said, was to discuss a means of paying the money.

I hadn't a penny with me, and that's the truth. Some people believe that I handed over the ransom for Ben in the shed, but that's a myth. In effect, all I wanted was to get a note to Ben to let him know that we were all concerned about him and praying for him, to establish somehow that these were the people who were holding him, and then to find out how to advance this thing. So we talked. They wanted me to bring the money up, but I said I wasn't prepared to do that. To be honest with you, I didn't really give a damn about the amount of money they were looking for, but I said that I couldn't personally hand it over because I couldn't have it on my conscience if it was used to buy arms. I said I couldn't do it and I wouldn't do it, but I added 'I would be prepared to enter into some kind of a brokerage whereby some of the money could be left somewhere for you, and then when Ben is released, we can see what's possible from there.

Although he was wearing his clerical collar, none of the kidnappers referred to McCarthy as 'Father', leading him to wonder whether they were loyalist paramilitaries. In that part of the world it was highly unlikely, but McCarthy asked them for proof that they really had his friend.

I said to them, 'I have no guarantee that you are holding Ben. I don't know who I'm doing business with here, and if there's any business to be done.' One thing was certain, I didn't want to be a patsy. I felt I had some bargaining power because they needed an intermediary. They were able to describe Ben in a way that made it clear to me that they had him. They weren't too forthcoming when I asked how he was being kept. Was he blindfolded, did he have a radio, was anyone with him? But I asked whether I could write a note to him and they said I could. I had a biro and a piece of paper with me. I just wanted to let him know that his family was okay, that Mary was alright; obviously we were all worried and we were doing our best to get a solution. I wrote the note and asked them would they give it to him, and they said they would. Then it was back to how do we advance this thing.

It was quite straightforward. There was money there. There were plenty of people who loved Ben enough to want to pay it, friends and family. I wasn't prepared to touch the money, but I said that between us we could come up with a way of getting it to them. Every now and then the two senior guys – the one in charge and the second-in-command – would leave the shed to discuss a point I'd made, and leave the man with the radio with me. I think he was the heavy. Then they'd come back and I'd be asked further questions. It was the number two who conducted all the questioning, under the direction of the leader. On one occasion the three of them went outside, because we were very near to coming to a deal. And as they were standing just outside the open door of the shed, a shot hit the wall near the door. And then another one. And I heard, 'Jesus!' and they returned fire. They had rifles. The third guy tore back into the shed, grabbed the radio, which he'd left lying on the floor, and they ran.

At around 5pm, two Gardaí from the Special Task Force and a young soldier were searching an area around Roche Castle – a thirteenth-century Norman ruin on a rocky hilltop that once controlled a pass into Armagh – when they spotted masked men in the distance, talking outside the shed. One of the Gardaí shouted a warning. There was an exchange of fire and the men escaped on foot across a field to the other side of the border.

I took cover. I was down on my hunkers, behind a wall, and I can remember so many things being in my head at the one time. First of all, stupidly, the Kojak series was on television at the time and I remember saying to myself, 'What would Kojak do in this situation?' The second was to say an Act of Contrition. Third was a real worry that the kidnappers might have thought I set them up and led the police to them, and I was lucky that I didn't stop a bullet before they ran off. The other thing on my mind was that I still didn't know whether I was north or south of the border. I didn't know whether the people coming were RUC and British army or Special Branch and Irish army. It makes a difference, I felt.

Now, if you can picture the scene where I was. I was in a shed, and opposite me, across a yard, there was a series of two-storey stone farm buildings with steps going up the outside of them, no window panes, just open holes. I didn't know whether the three gunmen were hiding out in there or not, but if they were cornered there, I was a sitting duck, along with the security personnel. It's now dusk and the light is sinking fast. I came to the door of the shed and I stood there quietly, and coming towards me to my left were two plainclothes men and a soldier. The detectives had pistols and the soldier had a rifle.

They didn't see me at first. They walked across my line of vision, looking in the direction that the three had run, guns pointed in front of them. I coughed and the three of them spun around, and there I was, standing in the doorway. That was the most frightening moment. The young soldier can't have been any more than twenty or twenty-one. Perspiration was rolling off him. He was clearly scared out of his wits. I was really afraid he'd lose it if I made any slight movement or something. I said to him, as gently as I could, 'Would you ever put that thing down? I'm not a kidnapper. They're gone.' One of the detectives snapped at me, 'Where did they go?' I said, 'I don't know. They disappeared somewhere.' I was told to put my hands over my head, which I did. But I thought I could handle the situation now because I heard their accents and realised I was still south of the border. I told them I was Dermod McCarthy, Father Dermod McCarthy, and I was here trying to get negotiations going. 'Come out,' they said. They took me away from the shed. I had to climb over a five-barred gate with barbed wire across the top and I tore my coat in the process. Come to think of it, Ben still owes me a new coat!

The soldier went off searching for the three kidnappers and the detectives stayed with me. One of them gave his gun to the other and he started to search me. He found the apple in my pocket. He said, 'Who touched that apple?' I said, 'Who touched the apple? Just me. Oh, and one of the kidnappers when he was searching me.' So he left it there in my pocket.

They were querying and questioning me, and I could tell they didn't believe my story. They asked me where I was from and I said, originally Ballinamore. They immediately stiffened and exchanged looks, I presume because that region of south Leitrim close to the Border was a well-known republican hotbed. But I'd nothing to do with it. I was looking at one of the detectives and said to myself, 'That face looks familiar.' I asked him, 'Have you a sister, Breda?' Of course that made things worse, because the families of detectives who were involved in these kinds of things were being threatened at the time, and he thought I had a line on him. He said, 'Why do you want to know that?' I said, 'Did PJ and herself enjoy meeting the Pope last week?' He said, 'How do you know that?' and I said, 'Because I arranged the audience in Rome for them.'

The detective was Declan Brogan, a brother-in-law of PJ Mara, Charles Haughey's press secretary when Fianna Fáil were in government. The connection helped lighten the atmosphere, but within minutes the air was filled with the sound of helicopters, and hundreds of Gardaí and soldiers who were combing the remote terrain around the border rushed to the scene. All routes across the border to Crossma-glen and Foxhill were sealed off, but the men were already out of the Republic and back in the relative sanctuary of South Armagh. Senior Gardaí weren't convinced by McCarthy's story. He drove back to Dundalk under a heavy escort to be questioned. The apple, a piece of evidence that could potentially lead the authorities to the kidnappers, was still in McCarthy's pocket.

> Would you believe, I ate the darned apple on the way to Dundalk! I was starving, and it never dawned on me, of course, that the gunmen had touched it and the Gardaí might want to fingerprint it. I can't remember if the one who searched me was wearing gloves at the time or not. It could have been the best lead the Gardaí had, and I ate it. They were furious with me, and I can't blame them. I was still a suspect at that stage. They'd established that I was a priest, but I think they thought I was one of those IRA priests. A few clergy over the years have been a bit too involved in the whole IRA move-ment, unwisely in my view, and then, coming from the part of the country that I did, it was only natural that they'd think that. They questioned me at length in Dundalk and I gave a statement. They let me go late on Sunday evening and I drove back to Dublin to tell Mary I'd met Ben's kidnappers and they said her husband was doing fine. The thing that made me sad subsequently was finding out that Ben got a hiding that night.

One of the gang went to Dunne that night and told him, 'One of our fellas nearly got shot on account of you,' and he was beaten up while he was hooded and his arms tied behind his back. When the adrenalin of the night subsided, they read him McCarthy's letter. It said: 'Ben. Thinking, working and praying very hard for you. Keep your chin up. Mary is fine and sends her love and the children are fine. May God bless you. Dermod.'

❖❖❖

The shoot-out at Castleroche highlighted tensions between the police on either side of the border. The Gardaí were dismayed by the pace of the investigation in the North. It was believed that Dunne was held at a farmhouse somewhere within a ten-mile radius of Crossmaglen, and still there was no success in finding him. The RUC were never slow to point out that the IRA enjoyed a safe sanctuary along the Republic side of the border, much to the embarrassment of the Gardaí. But here were three gunmen who fired at members of the Republic's security forces and escaped to the safety of the North, an area that was, in effect, unpoliced after dark. Garret FitzGerald phoned the British Ambassador, Sir Leonard Figg, to say it was unacceptable that South Armagh was in the control of the IRA at night.

On Monday morning, 20 October, McCarthy met Fox and Freaney at Freaney's office in Dublin and gave them an account of his all too brief talks with the kidnappers. He told them that, before the ambush, the gang had agreed in principle to his suggestion that a substantial portion of the ransom be 'left somewhere' and they would 'see what else was possible' after Dunne's release. Undeterred by his close encounter with death the night before, McCarthy decided to drive back to north Louth in an effort to re-establish communication with the gang. Knowing that the place was likely to be under surveillance, he left Freaney's office in the boot of a car and was dropped at Jury's Hotel in Ballsbridge. He went in through the front door and left immediately by an entrance at the back, where he had arranged for another car, a Renault 16, to be waiting.

I went back up again towards the border because I was very anxious to find out where Ben was and who among the young people of the area would know what was going down. I later had a conversation with the Garda Commissioner, who told me I behaved in a foolhardy way, and he was right. But at the time our only concern was saving Ben's life. So I headed up in the dark blue Renault, which was the 'Radharc' car. Now, as it happened, I had a perfect cover story for going up. Some time before that I had done a film on the return visit of young Irish people to the Pope in 1981. A lot of diocese around the country who'd participated were anxious to get their hands on copies of the film. This was back in the days when VCRs were uncommon. So I rang the priest who was in charge of youth affairs in the Diocese of Armagh, and I asked to meet him to talk about the number and distribution of copies for his diocese. We agreed to meet at the parochial house in Ardee, County Louth. The local curate was there and so was the parish priest. The four of us ended up having tea together and the whole topic of conversation was a report in that morning's newspaper about a shootout on the border and a priest being involved. They were speculating among themselves about who it might have been, and, of course, I added my own little bit.

After tea, I went into another room with the Youth Director and I said to him, 'Forget about the Pope videos. That's not why I'm here. I'm here about the conversation that took place at the table out there. I was the priest yesterday.' His reaction was, 'Mother of

Divine God! What are you walking me into?' I said to him, 'Look, you're in touch with young people in the area of South Armagh. We know that Ben is being held there, somewhere close to the border. I'm not asking you to name names, but I'm asking you to keep your eyes open and to quietly see if any unusual goings-on could point us to where Ben is being kept.' He said that the kind of youth activities he was involved with were youth leadership projects, weekend retreats, football and so forth and he didn't tend to hear things of that nature. He said he'd keep his ears open, but didn't expect to find out anything that would be of use to me.

As a result of all his security precautions, McCarthy had managed to drive to Ardee without being followed. But his luck ran out when he pulled over in the town to ask for directions to the parochial house. The man he stopped was a plainclothes Garda inspector, who recognised him and immediately tipped off the Special Branch. When he was a mile outside Ardee on his return journey, two squad cars appeared in his rear view mirror and flashed their headlights to get him to pull over. The priest was ordered out of his car and into the back of one of the squad cars. The Gardaí suspected that McCarthy had dropped off the ransom at the parochial house for the IRA to collect, and that the drop was prearranged in the shed at Castleroche the previous night.

I was sat in the back of a squad car, jammed between two detectives. I realised pretty quickly that they still had their suspicions about me from what had happened the previous day, and they hadn't fully bought my story. 'What were you doing in that house,' I was asked. I said I was meeting another priest to discuss distribution of 'The Return Visit' in the Armagh diocese. The detective said,

'Come off it,' and I said, 'Okay, you know who I am and you know what this is about. I was asking someone who knows a lot of young people in the area of South Armagh to keep his eyes open for anything unusual.' He said, 'You want to do our job, is that it?' I said, 'Not at all, but every little bit helps.' He said, 'Who else was in the house?' I said, 'Just the parish priest, the curate of the parish, the diocesan Youth Director and myself. And there was a housekeeper as well, who made tea for us.' He said, 'Who else was there?' His voice was getting louder. Again I said 'Nobody that I know of.' He said, 'You better tell us who else was there or it could be very serious for you.' It began to get heavy. I kept protesting that I didn't know of anyone else in the house, and for the first time I began to understand how people feel when they get the sharp end of the police when they're innocent. You feel totally alone. You're answering their questions truthfully, but they don't believe you. My father was a Garda, and you always had the sense that they were on your side. This was one of those times when I didn't feel that. They told me they had plenty of time to sit there until I told them who else was in the house. After what seemed like an age of the same question being asked and the same reply being given, along with veiled dire threats if I didn't tell the truth, I asked, 'How can you be so sure someone else was there?' and one of them said, 'Whose was the Northern registration car outside?' Then I said, 'Hold on a minute. The curate who was there is not long in the parish; I think he came from somewhere up around Lough Neagh. He might still have the same car he had when he was there.' They got on the radio and checked it out, and that was in fact what had happened. They let me go then. I shook all the way back to Dublin and was very glad to get home that night.

❖❖❖

Republican sources have confirmed what senior Gardaí have long suspected, that the IRA received £300,000 for Dunne, though it's not clear how it was handed over. As McCarthy said, a lot of things were happening all over the place and there were so many cars leaving Dublin that week that the Gardaí will never know whether any of them contained the ransom. But another effort to pay it was foiled that Monday night, when the RUC stopped two southern registered cars at a checkpoint just outside Bambridge on the main Newry to Belfast road. Both cars were carrying a substantial amount of money in Irish punts; they were escorted back to the border.

At about the same time, the three vehicles used in the kidnapping were found burnt out in a field in Forkhill, close to the border in South Armagh. Just after 6pm, the blue Transit van, the Opel Ascona and the motorbike that was used to follow Dunne across the border and to check on McCarthy in Louth village, were placed together in a field and set alight. Nobody saw anything suspicious, which was far from unusual in South Armagh. The RUC took it as evidence that the IRA were feeling the heat of the searches around Crossmaglen and Cullyhanna.

The Gardaí were annoyed with the Dunne family, not just because of their efforts to pay the ransom, but because there had been no public appeal for Ben's release. A tearful wife or mother will often tug at the conscience of someone who knows something. Mary Dunne's only public utterance so far was to assure the kidnappers that the family was doing all it could to hand over the money. On Tuesday, Dermod McCarthy was called into Garda Headquarters in the Phoenix Park in Dublin for a meeting. He was given a dressing down for his meddling and asked why none of the family had simply asked the kidnappers to give Dunne back. After the meeting he phoned Mary, but she was too upset to make a television appeal and asked McCarthy to do it instead. McCarthy recalls:

> I rang Tom McCaughran in RTÉ, whom I knew, and I asked him to come out to the Dunne house on Wednesday morning. And he filmed and recorded an appeal by me to the kidnappers. I considered very carefully what I said. Then McCaughren and his crew tore across Dublin through the city traffic to get it out on the one o'clock radio news. The kidnappers heard it. Ben heard it. It was on every radio in the house where he was being held. It went out on RTÉ, Downtown Radio, BBC, all over the place, repeated every hour in every bulletin.

In his appeal to the kidnappers, McCarthy said: 'I know you to be shrewd, intelligent men. I appeal to you, in the name of God and in the name of common sense. Cut your losses now, release Ben and get out while you still have time.' Dunne later described McCarthy's words as being 'like manna from heaven,' working like some magic incantation on the kidnappers. But it was odd how McCarthy's apparently innocuous message suddenly snapped the IRA gang to its senses. 'I have no doubt that the appeal brought home to them that people were zooming in on all sides, and now was the time to get out,' Dunne recalled after his release. Others scanned the message for a hidden trigger that told the IRA the money had been delivered. 'That interpretation was put on it at one stage, but it was untrue,' says McCarthy.

> There was a kind of code in the appeal, and it was, 'Get out while you still have time.' In other words, get out before you're kneecapped by your own people. Because I had put out some inquiries about what was actually happening, and I was told that the group that kidnapped Ben was a breakaway group. And what I was told at the time was that the Army Council of the IRA were becoming furious with them, because, in the process of trying to find Ben, it was as if a basket was being upturned and every hidden bomb and bullet along the border was being discovered. There were hidden caches of arms being found all over the place, and this was really getting up the noses of the IRA leadership, who hadn't authorised this. This is the information I had when I recorded the appeal for radio on Wednesday morning.

Republican sources at the time blamed the kidnapping on the twenty-strong maverick unit known as the Edentubber Group, which was said to be led by a former senior IRA figure who was disillusioned with the lack of Provisional activity around the south Down border. Edentubber was a small townland in South Armagh with a population of just twenty-six, and, it was said, just one able-bodied resident between the ages of fifteen and sixty. The unit adopted the name because of the local memorial to five Volunteers killed in a 1957 bomb blast that acted as their rallying point.

It's not strictly true to say that the operation was unsanctioned, since the unit, like many others in South Armagh, enjoyed a degree of autonomy, always operating on the understanding that what they were doing had the approval of the leadership. But now they were bringing a huge amount of security force attention to the sensitive border area. According to republican sources, not long before Mc Carthy's appeal, the gang had been ordered to release Dunne and to get out of the area.

At 9.30pm one of the gang went to Dunne and said, 'We've good news for you. You won't have to sleep in the fields. You're being released.' The gunmen's abrupt decision to let him go could be because he had become 'too hot to handle', or in response to an order from the IRA leadership. But there is another possible reason – that they got paid that night. Late on Wednesday afternoon, a courier is understood to have left Dublin in a white Ford Escort with a large sum of money. The Gardaí found out about this latest attempt to make the ransom drop when the car was already on the main Dublin to Belfast road, and their efforts to find it were hampered by the huge crowd that were converging on Dundalk that night for a football match. Dundalk were playing Tottenham Hotspur in the European Cup Winners Cup, and the driver of the car took advantage of the bedlam on the roads leading into and out of the town to slip unnoticed over the border.

Dunne gave no sign of his relief and happiness when he was told he was to be freed. 'I was playing my cards close to my chest,' he said later. Shortly before midnight, still tied and hooded, he was bundled into the back of a car and driven at what he recalled as a rate of knots through the Armagh countryside, with all the car windows open and guns at the ready. Having spent six days silently praying to be found, what he feared most at that point was a rescue attempt.

They drove for about twenty minutes and arrived in a churchyard. Dunne was pushed out into the bitter night air, had his hood removed and was told not to turn around. If he saw the licence plate of the car, he was told, they would have no choice but to shoot him. A member of the gang handed him three bullets. One was from the revolver of the man who guarded him. The other two were from an Armalite rifle, one a souvenir for him, the other for the priest who had put his neck on the block for him.

'There'll be someone along in twenty minutes,' one of the gang said. Dunne stood on a high spot in the churchyard that looked out on the lights of the smattering of houses that make up the village of Cullyhanna in South Armagh. When he heard the car disappear, he was overcome by a sudden panic attack. Convinced that the gunmen were about to return for him, he jumped into a grave that had been freshly dug for a funeral the following morning.

Eamonn Mallie, a journalist with Downtown Radio, received a phone call shortly after midnight. A voice said, 'The man who is missing can be picked up at Cullyhanna Parochial House.' Mallie got there within twenty minutes and found Dunne, looking dazed and shaken. Father Hugh O'Neill, the parish priest, took them in and Dunne had a bottle of ale to unwind, then phoned McCarthy to ask him to break the news of his release gently to his family. Mallie then drove him across the border and back to Dublin. It was only when he was less than an hour from home that Dunne allowed himself to believe that it was over. He asked Mallie to pull over and he called Mary from a phone box. Then, tired, traumatised and thrown by the suddenness with which his ordeal ended, he went home.

❖❖❖

Ben Dunne has spoken publicly about his ordeal in only the barest details. His most candid account of his days in captivity and how he survived came in a speech he gave at a thanksgiving Mass held in the Pro-Cathedral on 9 November. He said:

'I don't want to seem like a hypocrite or some kind of Holy Joe. This is the first time that I've ever stood up and talked in a church. But I would like you to know that there were two overpowering feelings I experienced during those six days.

'Number one – communication. I felt like I was speaking to Him (*he pointed upwards*) directly. I fought with Him. I praised Him. I argued with Him. I said 'What did I do to deserve this?' But I had an experience of talking to Him and He listening and hearing me, as if He were on the other end of a telephone. Call it prayer if you like, but I now have no doubt that He listens and hears us when we want to talk to Him.

'Number two – the second thing following on from the first. He gave me an unbelieveable strength and a certainty in my mind that even if they'd shot me, it wasn't the end, I became absolutely certain of life after death, that if I died – and at times I really thought they would kill me – I would eventually meet my wife and children again and that took away any fear of death. And I'm not afraid of it anymore. For that I thank God.'

CHAPTER FIVE

Shoot-Out at Derrada Wood
Don Tidey's Ordeal

'You're taking people who aren't actually involved in the conflict and you're holding them hostage and you've got their wives and daughters and sons on the television, crying their hearts out. It costs you sympathy and support.' An IRA source

The IRA had expected to be well in funds in 1983 as a result of the Shergar kidnapping. But that episode, more like the plot of a Dick Francis novel than a serious IRA operation, had been a fiasco, and they came away with nothing. They were so desperate for money now that by early summer of 1983 they were already planning another kidnapping. This time there was no room for gimmicks. It was decided to revisit the success of the Dunne operation with the back-to-basics abduction of a wealthy supermarket boss.

The target this time was Galen Weston, the forty-two-year-old Canadian billionaire whose interests included the Quinnsworth and Penneys chains and the exclusive Brown Thomas department store in Dublin. The team for the job was picked from Kevin Mallon's Special Operations unit. They were all in their late twenties or early thirties and included Gerry Fitzgerald, John Stewart and John Hunter, all from Northern Ireland but living in Ballybough on the north side of Dublin. Peter Lynch, a bricklayer from Dungiven, County Derry, and Nicky Kehoe, an unemployed bricklayer from Cabra in Dublin who, like Lynch, had previously served time for possessing explosives, were also in on the job. They spent a few weeks, on and off, watching Weston and his Irish wife Hilary come and go from their secluded mansion in Roundwood, County Wicklow, before choosing 7 August 1983 as the date for the kidnapping.

But the plan was betrayed by Sean O'Callaghan, the high level informer in the IRA's southern command. O'Callaghan, a twenty-nine-year-old Volunteer from Tralee, County Kerry, had been passing valuable information about operations to the Gardaí for years. At the beginning of the summer, he told his handler that none of the Special Operations Team seconded to Mallon for the Shergar operation had returned to regular duties, and it was likely that they were planning another major kidnapping. He gave the Gardaí the names of the unit members he knew and the address of the safe house in Dublin where the operation was planned. From surveillance and telephone taps the full picture began to emerge.

Weston was visited by two Special Branch detectives, who told him the IRA were planning to abduct him, and suggested that he and Hilary discreetly leave the country. They went to England, where they had a house at Windsor, close to the royal castle. At 6pm on 6 August, Weston was playing polo with his friend, Prince Charles, when a detective phoned John O'Sullivan, the farm manager on his Roundwood estate, and told him to expect a party of Gardaí. Half an hour later, the house and grounds were crawling with plainclothes Gardaí armed with Uzi subma-chine guns and revolvers. They had already studied the layout of the house and decided from maps where best to place themselves to ambush the kidnap gang, who were expected at dawn the following morning.

Late that night they took up their positions. Detective Inspector John O'Mahony, who was in charge of the opera-tion, was in the main house. Detective Garda Delaney climbed up onto the roof. Detective Garda Kevin Lynch was located in O'Sullivan's house. Detective Sergeant Walter Rice took up a position in the garage facing the courtyard. The rest were scattered about the place.

Just after 4am, O'Mahony heard a tinkling sound from the phone in the living room, a sign that the telephone wires had been cut. He picked up the phone and there was no dial tone. The operation had begun. At 5.30am, O'Sullivan and his wife were told to go to their son's room at the back of their house and barricade themselves in. They leaned a mat-tress against the wall and huddled together underneath, bracing themselves for the shooting to start. Outside, the kidnap team checked their weapons. Stewart and Hunter had Belgian-made Vigneron submachine guns, popular with the Italian police. Fitzgerald had a Gustav submachine gun, the kind used by the Irish army. Kehoe had a Browning automatic pistol and Lynch an old-fashioned Webley revolver that was later found to be unloaded. Two, or possi-bly three, other Volunteers covered them from a position on a hill that overlooked the house.

At 7.15am Delaney caught the first sight of the gang from his own position on the roof. He saw two figures on the hill.

They gave a signal and were joined by six others. Five approached the gates of the house, which were unlocked. Two entered the courtyard first, followed by three more, all of them wearing masks and different coloured boiler suits. Gardaí inside the main house heard one of the gang ask, 'Is it safe? Is it fucking safe? Is it fucking safe?' Then they heard, 'We're going in.' When he saw the men, Rice, who was in the garage, shouted, 'Gardaí. Drop your guns,' and fired a warning shot into the air. One of the gang shouted, 'Come on, ye bastards,' and there was an exchange of shots. From his position in O'Sullivan's house, Detective Garda Lynch heard the sounds of shouts and shooting. He smashed a window and let off a burst of fire from his submachine gun, forcing two of the gang to dive for cover behind a low wall.

The five Volunteers were easily overcome. In their shock, only Hunter and Kehoe had managed to fire a shot during what became a one-sided gun battle. The Gardaí let off almost two hundred rounds. Four of the gang were injured. Stewart and Fitzgerald were hit outside the garage. Fitzgerald was bleeding heavily from a bullet wound to his arm. Fearing he was about to die, he asked a Garda to say an Act of Contrition in his ear, which he did. Fitzgerald repeated the words after him. Kehoe, the only one of the gang who wasn't hit, was overpowered. Hunter and Lynch tried to escape through an alleyway, but were too badly wounded to get far. Lynch, who was shot in the head, was lying face-down, apparently dead, when Detective Garda Thomas Connolly found him. Hunter was sitting propped up against a wall a few yards away, still clutching his submachine gun. Connolly shouted at him to drop his weapon, which he did before peeling off his balaclava. He was hand-cuffed and searched. Lynch was losing a lot of blood. Another Garda said an Act of Contrition into his ear and told him that an ambulance was on its way. The four were taken to hospital under heavy armed guard. Kehoe was brought to Dublin for questioning. The men on the hill, who, O'Callaghan later alleged, included Mallon himself, got away.

On Thursday, 3 November 1983, the five men were found guilty of firearms offences and each was sentenced to between ten and fourteen years in prison. It was an expensive disaster for the Provisionals. Shergar had only cost the organisation prestige; the Weston operation cost them five operatives. Mallon might not have got the opportunity to fail again were it not for the arrest of Ivor Bell, the IRA chief of staff, on 9 September that year. Bell and twenty-seven others were picked up by the RUC, who were acting on the word of Belfast Brigade adjutant Robert Lean, the latest so-called supergrass, who agreed to testify against his former comrades. Lean later retracted his evidence. But because of his arrest, Bell lost his rank, and Kevin McKenna, an old ally of Mallon's from the Tyrone brigade, became the IRA chief of staff.

❖❖❖

The IRA intended demanding a large seven-figure sum for Weston, and now they were determined to get the money from him by another means. Mallon set his sights on one of Weston's senior executives, but told very few people the identity of the intended target. The ambush in

Roundwood confirmed what the IRA had suspected for a long time, that an informant was working at a senior level within the organisation. This time Mallon was determined to be cautious; the only person in whom he confided, O'Callaghan later claimed, was Pat Currie, a Belfast republican who he knew from their time in Portlaoise together. According to O'Callaghan, Currie, who moved to Tralee, County Kerry after his release, was enlisted to help plan the kidnapping. With most of the Special Operations team in jail, O'Callaghan was asked to supply four men and a clean car for the job. He put forward the names of Mick Burke, a Volunteer from Cork; another Volunteer from County Clare, who had served time in prison in Belfast on explosives charges, and two Tralee men who had raised money for the IRA locally with raids on hotels, shops and factories. Two stolen cars would be used in the kidnapping, but they also needed a hire car that could pass through Garda checkpoints unsuspected. O'Callaghan asked Billy Kelly, a forty-year-old painter and republican sympathiser from just outside Tralee, to hire the car, which he did.

O'Callaghan could tell the Gardaí a lot about the operation, but not the name of the target. The snatch team weren't told until the night before, and even then it's unlikely they would have ever heard of Don Tidey. Despite being the chairman and chief executive of Quinnsworth, the largest supermarket chain in the country, Tidey was barely known to the public, preferring to keep a lower profile than other retail bosses like Ben Dunne and Fergal Quinn. Tidey was an easy-going, quixotic, forty-nine year-old widower and father of three. When he had moved to Dublin from his native England some years before, he found work in Dunnes Stores. Two years later he moved to Quinnsworth and progressed to the top of the career ladder. He lived with his children in a modern dormer bungalow in Woodtown Way, a cul-de-sac of ten houses in Rathfarnham, just south of Dublin. Tidey was fastidious about his routines. He was ready for work at 7.40am every morning and, more often than not, was left waiting in the hallway for Susan, his thirteen-year-old daughter, whom he dropped to school at Alexandra College in Milltown on his way to the office.

The gang arrived outside the estate after just after 6am on Thursday, 24 November. They had two cars: a beige Ford Cortina stolen the night before from the parish clerk of Newcastlewest, County Limerick, and a Ford Escort, stolen in Kerry some weeks earlier and hidden in a lock-up garage in Tralee. At his usual time, Tidey swung his Daimler out of the driveway, while Alistair, one of his sons, who also worked for Quinnsworth, followed in his own car. As they turned out of the estate on Stocking Lane, they ran straight into what looked like a roadblock. A Cortina with a flashing blue light on its roof was pulled up at the side of the road, alongside a Ford Escort. Tidey wondered if there had been an accident. Burke, wearing a Garda uniform, flagged him down. Tidey opened his window and Burke produced a submachine gun, which he put to his head. Tidey tried to put his car into reverse, but in his panic he only managed to grind the gears. A number of shots were fired into the air as a warning. A member of the gang opened the front passenger door and dragged Susan out onto the road, while another went to the car behind and forced Alistair to hand over his keys. Tidey was dragged into the back of the Cortina and driven off at high speed. Another member of the gang took the Daimler, which was later found dumped, with its tyres slashed. The rest of the gang escaped in the Escort, the whole convoy tearing up Stocking Lane in the direction of the Dublin Mountains.

The kidnappers took the steep and snaking Old Court Road to avoid the rush-hour traffic and drove to Maynooth, County Kildare. The rendezvous point was Connolly's Folly, a striking eighteenth-century obelisk on the outskirts of the town, where a second gang was waiting to take Tidey north to Ballinamore, County Leitrim. The plan, it seems, was to dump the two stolen cars and drive the original snatch team back to Tralee in the hire car before they were missed. But, according to O'Callaghan's account, they hit a snag. On his way to the rendezvous, he claimed, Currie crashed the car that Kelly had rented and then tried unsuccessfully to burn it out. Burke, the Clareman and the two Tralee men had no option but to travel to Ballinamore with the second team, which was made up of a handful of Volunteers from Leitrim and at least two of the thirty-eight IRA prisoners who had escaped from the Maze Prison in a hijacked food lorry in September. The Cortina was dumped and the Escort set alight. The two gangs then headed north in a brown Renault 12, a yellow mini and a red Commer van, with their prisoner tied up and blindfolded in the back of the van.

The quickest route to Ballinamore would have taken them through Mullingar, Longford and Carrick-on-Shannon. When they reached Ballinamore they continued north to Derrada, where Tidey – bound, blindfolded and with cotton wool now taped over his ears – was marched through thick briars and undergrowth into the middle of a dense wood, where it was planned to hide him. A bunker had been constructed out of polythene and wood in a ridge in the sloping ground. It was fifteen feet in length, four feet wide and five feet high. The plastic kept the rain off but did nothing to insulate Tidey and his guards from the bitter winter cold. But they presumed Tidey's bosses would pay up quickly and they would soon be out of there.

❖❖❖

There were very serious misgivings about the kidnapping within the IRA leadership. 'The reaction of a fair few of us was, "Have we learned nothing?" says one senior figure. It was, "Here we go again." Everything fucking ripped up. Safe houses, arms dumps, the lot.' And there was also the unspoken fear that operations like the Tidey kidnapping would, sooner or later, bring the Provisionals into conflict with the heavily armed Garda Special Task Force, which was set up in 1980 to target paramilitaries who were involved in bank robberies. The IRA's general army order number eight forbade any act of aggression against the security forces in the Republic. The shootout in Roundwood had already been a breach of that. 'It was clear that things were getting out of hand,' says one British intelligence source from the time.

It shows how much of a low ebb their finances were at. The problem for them was that they couldn't really do these operations in the North; it was just more difficult to operate there. But doing these kinds of things in the Republic, you could see it was only going to bring the security forces down there down on top of them. I mean, this was at the height of the Troubles, when they needed safe havens. And let's be honest, the Republic was a relatively safe area to operate from, especially the border counties. From Dundalk all the way up to Donegal there was an acquiescence. The only Rubicon that wasn't to be crossed was getting involved in conflict with the Garda Síochána and the Irish Army. And, with the Tidey kidnapping, they crossed the Rubicon.

Garret FitzGerald's government stuck to the same rigid line it took during the Dunne kidnapping – Tidey's family and his employers were to be stopped from handing over money for his return. Intelligence estimates said that the £5m the IRA wanted for him would be enough to re-arm and cover their operating costs for two years. The minister for justice, Michael Noonan, told the Dáil: 'The probable cost of it in terms of human life and suffering does not need to be spelled out.'

By lunchtime on the day of the kidnapping, the Gardaí and the army had set up roadblocks on all exit roads out of Dublin, but they suspected that they were already too late. Disused buildings on the islands in Lough Mask, County Mayo, and Lough Corrib, County Galway, were searched after a tip-off, but nothing was found. There were also searches in Leitrim, close to its borders with County Donegal and County Fermanagh. But Tidey and the IRA gang were secreted so deep inside the vast woods at Derrada that they weren't going to be found without an informant pinpointing exactly where they were hiding.

❖❖❖

The IRA could be grateful that the kidnapping had happened at a time when security co-operation between the police forces on either side of the border was practically non-existent. There was a long history of friction between the two, especially over RUC claims that some Gardaí were soft on the IRA. Garda Commissioner Laurence Wren – the man who had accepted Eddie Gallagher's surrender eight years earlier – was at loggerheads with RUC Chief Constable Sir John Hermon over his refusal to launch a public inquiry into the so-called Dowra affair. In 1981, Tom Nangle, a Garda who happened to be the brother-in-law of Fianna Fáil's minister for justice, Sean Doherty, was alleged to have assaulted Jimmy McGovern, a republican from Fermanagh, at a pub in Blacklion, County Cavan. On 27 September 1982, the day he was due to cross the border to give evidence in the District court in Dowra, McGovern was arrested by the RUC. When McGovern failed to show up in court, the case collapsed. Hours later, he was released without charge. There were allegations of collusion and of efforts by RUC officers to pervert the course of justice in the Republic, and FitzGerald remained furious about it.

❖❖❖

A constant stream of friends came and went from the Tidey home over the weekend, offering help and sympathy. Susan was deeply traumatised by what had happened. Her father, it turned out, had warned the family about the possibility that he would be kidnapped. After the attempt to abduct

Galen Weston, all supermarket executives had been advised by the Gardaí to review their personal security. Tidey knew he was at particular risk because, like Ben Dunne, he regularly travelled to and from the North, where he was also chief executive of the Stewarts supermarket chain. Andrew recalled his father trying to prepare them for the eventuality and assuring them that he was strong enough to survive what Dunne went through. Physically, he was fit. He was a keen runner and regularly tackled the hills around Mount Venus and the Hellfire Club in the Dublin Mountains. Spiritually, he was tough too. He was a regular churchgoer and had a strong faith, which he tended to fall back on during difficult periods in his life. 'We have great confidence in his strength,' Andrew said. 'He's a great runner, a health food fanatic, very religious and determined.'

Officially, the ransom demand for Tidey – £5million – was phoned to the London offices of Associated British Foods, Quinnsworth's Weston-owned parent company, on Sunday, 27 November, three days after the kidnapping, but it's thought likely that there was earlier contact. As in the Shergar case, the kidnappers wanted all of the negotiations to be conducted outside the State. But the British police agreed to a Garda request to tap the home and office lines of all senior ABF executives, to stop a deal being cut.

❖❖❖

The amount of money the IRA wanted was chickenfeed to the Weston family. Their business, credited, among other things, with introducing sliced bread to Britain in the 1930s, was one of the biggest companies in Europe, achieving sales of almost £3bn sterling in 1982. Under Galen's brother, Garry, ABF grew from a million pound to a billion pound concern during the 1970s, buoyed by the popularity of its Allinson and Kingsmill bread brands and its manufacture of Ryvita crackers and Silver Spoon sugar, not to mention the invention of the 'Wagon Wheel' biscuit

The fortune inherited by the Weston brothers was made by their grandfather, George Weston, the son of a cockney who moved to Canada during the nineteenth century. He set up a bakery. His motto, according to family legend, was: 'People will eat horseshit if it has enough icing on it.' It was his son, Garfield – Galen and Garry's father – who started the process of turning the Weston business into a multinational conglomerate, bringing his novel, ready-cut loaves to Britain in 1934. Within five years the company had thirty bakeries in Britain and had pioneered the first low-priced tea biscuit, up until then a luxury that only the middle classes could afford.

After the Second World War, the company spread its tentacles into the United States, Australia, South Africa and Ireland, where it set up the Power's supermarket chain. In 1951 they acquired a controlling stake in the Queen's grocer, Fortnum & Mason. When Garfield handed over the business to his boys, Garry ran the British arm of the operation, while Galen looked after the family's Canadian and Irish interests, which now included the Quinnsworth supermarket chain, bought from Pat Quinn in 1972.

In personality Galen and Garfield were polar opposites. Galen was colourful and gregarious and he enjoyed pressing the flesh in elite social circles, especially among Britain's royals. Garry is remembered for his thrifty eccentricity as much for his philanthropy. He cut his children's hair, drove a secondhand car and regularly took the bus to work, as well as giving away tens of millions of pounds to charity.

Garry Weston's response to the IRA ransom demand was to say that ABF would abide by the Government's wishes, but the Gardaí suspected that a secret deal was being done. When the kidnappers phoned on Sunday they were asked to produce a recent photograph of Tidey as evidence that they were holding him and that he was alive. On Monday, 28 November, in his prison in Ballinamore, Tidey had his blindfold and earplugs removed and was handed a copy of that day's *Evening Herald* to hold up for a Polaroid shot, which was sent to ABF.

A number of Quinnsworth executives and senior staff were placed under Special Branch surveillance. On Tuesday, 29 November, at 11.15pm, armed detectives at Dublin Airport stopped the company's security manager, Des McSherry, from boarding a privately chartered plane to England with a briefcase containing a substantial sum of money. How much was never disclosed, although it couldn't have been more than a fraction of the £5m the IRA had demanded. Nonetheless, the Gardaí suspected that McSherry, who'd spent the previous day in England, was a key figure in a secret deal to buy Tidey's life. He was taken to Whitehall Garda Station, just north of the city, and held for questioning. When he was released the following morning, he was followed by the police back to Quinnsworth's head office in Dun Laoghaire Shopping Centre.

Garry Weston issued a statement after McSherry was

detained, insisting that his company was abiding by the Government's request: 'Following the abduction in the Irish Republic last week of Mr Don Tidey, one of our senior executives, my company has received demands for money to be paid over. The Gardaí have informed us that they believe the IRA is the organisation behind these demands. My company is aware that the Government has stated that it is opposed to the payment of ransom to terrorist organisations, and it has been specifically asked that this policy should be observed in this instance.

'With the life of a man at stake – one who is an admired and respected colleague – we stand ready to consider whatever is open to us to secure his safe release. But, notwithstanding our personal anxieties and concern, we feel we are bound – as must always be the case – by the overriding policy decisions of the governments concerned. I have been told that the security authorities of both British and Irish governments are doing all in their power to secure the outcome which we all so earnestly wish for. Until there is further news of Mr Tidey's well-being, the company – for obvious reasons – will not be adding to these comments.'

❖❖❖

The search for Don Tidey stretched the resources of the security forces to breaking point. At the time they were also looking for Dominic McGlinchey, the fugitive INLA leader who was on the run in the Republic, and for the bulk of the thirty-eight men who had recently shot their way out of the Maze prison. It is estimated that up to two-thirds of the entire Garda and army force may have been involved in the combined hunts, manning roadblocks, conducting house-to-house searches, and scouring vast tracts of countryside in four provinces.

Though the Gardaí had searched the border counties, the main focus of the hunt for Tidey was initially the southwest of the country. The kidnappers' ploy of using cars stolen in Kerry and Limerick had sent Gardaí in the wrong direction. By the time they did their usual sweeping up of known republicans in these areas on the day of the kidnapping, Burke and his three companions were supposed to be back in their homes with their alibis ready. But, because of the problem with the cars, they were still making their way back from Leitrim. O'Callaghan, who had passed all their names to the Gardaí, was visited in his flat that afternoon by Kelly, who was in a panic. The car he rented for the gang had been found, crashed and dumped, and both the Gardaí and the hire firm were looking for him. O'Callaghan didn't believe Kelly would have got involved had he known what the car was to be used for. He told him to report it as having been stolen; nothing could be proven. The two were arrested as they left the flat.

O'Callaghan regarded Kelly as a weak man who would buckle easily under questioning. Initially he stuck to his story that the car had been stolen on Wednesday, 23 November, the night before the kidnapping. During questioning on Friday afternoon he became unwell. He had a long-standing heart condition and was taken to St Catherine's Hospital, where Gardaí kept an armed vigil by his bedside overnight. By then they had enough on him. On Saturday night he was charged with falsely imprisoning

Tidey by unlawfully detaining him against his will. But it didn't bring the Gardaí any closer to finding the kidnappers. Kelly was just a low level functionary, and it was unlikely that he was let in on any of the details of the kidnapping.

❖❖❖

In the bunker in the woods in Derrada, Don Tidey devised a way of passing the time. In his imagination he loaded all of his memories into a filing cabinet. His wedding, the birth of his children, Christmases and birthdays were all put away under their own alphabetical headings. And whenever he thought he was losing his mind, he later told his friends, he'd open a drawer, pull out a file and savour that memory. It was his way of staying sane.

And others were thinking of him. Every night a vigil was held at the Church of Ireland church at Whitechurch, near Rathfarnham, where Tidey worshipped every week and where he was a member of the church choir. Every night, fifty or sixty parishioners gathered in the small granite church with an elegant spire, to sing hymns and pray for his safe return. The rector, Reverend Horace McKinley, one of Tidey's friends, prayed that 'the light of Christ may enter the hearts of those holding him.'

In each of the fifty-seven Quinnsworth supermarkets around the country there was a video appeal, asking shoppers who might have information to contact the Gardaí. As the first week passed, with no fresh news about his wellbeing, the Government came under increased emotional pressure to turn a blind eye to the ransom being paid. On

Thursday, 1 December – seven days after his father was taken – Andrew Tidey said in interview on the RTÉ news: 'We have now had to live for a week without my father and the strain has been quite terrible. The greatest worry is the silence. Every time the phone rings your hopes are raised, and when it isn't the kidnappers they are dashed.'

Garret FitzGerald recalls:

> It placed huge pressure on all of us in the Cabinet, the idea that this man had been snatched away from the family who loved him, and if we would only step aside and let this extremely wealthy multinational concern hand over the ransom, then he'd be set free and everything would be alright. That was the view of a lot of the public and I remember it was very difficult to argue against it at the time. But we had to keep reminding ourselves of the suffering and the loss of life that would result if we let this money get into the hands of the IRA.

Meanwhile, the search switched to north and west Donegal. Joint Garda and army checkpoints were set up near Dungloe and Gweedore, and houses in the Annagry and Ranafast areas were searched. When the brown Renault 12 used by the kidnappers was discovered dumped just outside Navan, it opened up another front in the hunt. Gardaí raided the homes of republicans in Meath and Kildare, while hundreds of square miles of countryside was searched in Roscommon, Mayo, Kerry and Limerick. But by the end of the second week some senior Gardaí were voicing private doubts about whether Tidey was still alive. If he was, their only real hope of getting him back was if they continued tearing up the border areas to put pressure on the

IRA leadership to order his release. The Provisionals still had nineteen Maze escapees on the run, most of them hiding in the Republic. A number of arms dumps had also been turned over, including a large concrete bunker in the garden of a house in Innishkeen, County Monaghan. It was accessed through a manhole and contained thousands of rounds of ammunition.

Weston and ABF appeared to be sticking by their word not to pay the ransom, although it is unlikely that the kidnappers would have kept Tidey alive into a third week if there wasn't at least some communication. But, as Christmas grew closer, with no fresh leads to report, his name dropped out of the news headlines. There were occasional revivals, such as when Tiede and Elisabeth Herrema arrived in Dublin in the middle of December. Despite their own ordeal, they'd decided to spend their retirement in Ireland, and they landed in the centre of another kidnap drama, this one directed by an old friend of Herrema's own captors. On Wednesday, 14 December, Herrema was asked to make a personal appeal to the IRA on RTÉ's early evening news. 'As far as I understand from the news in the papers,' he said, 'the ransom demand will not be paid. And from my own experience, I know what it means. The kidnappers should realise the consequences of their actions for themselves, for Mr Tidey, for his children and for Ireland as a nation. Only more pain can come from holding Mr Tidey.'

By then there had been a perceptible shift in the search activity, which had moved back towards Leitrim and the border with Fermanagh. The size of the Garda and army contingent that flooded the area suggested a major breakthrough in the investigation. On Tuesday, 13 December, three weeks to the day since Tidey was taken, more than a hundred Gardaí were removed from their normal duties and transferred to Carrick-on-Shannon, where they were joined by a convoy of army trucks and personnel from the fifty-eighth battalion based at Finner Camp, County Donegal. Checkpoints were set up on all roads leading into and out of Leitrim, with a heavy concentration of armed troops sealing off all main and minor roads across the border into Fermanagh. By Thursday afternoon, 15 December, the village of Ballinamore resembled a garrison town from civil war times, with hundreds of Gardaí and army personnel arriving in armoured cars, helicopters and buses. Searches were scaled down everywhere else in the country. They knew where the kidnappers were.

❖❖❖

In the normal run of events, Ballinamore would be one of the first ports of call for the Gardaí when they were hunting IRA men on the run. The village was little more than a speck on the map, less than thirty miles from the border, with a population of just 860. It was famous for three things: the desperately poor farmland that forced generations to emigrate; the nearby lakes that offered some of the best coarse fishing in western Europe; and its diehard support for the IRA, who were thought to have more safe houses in Ballinamore than in any town in the republic outside of Tralee. Its association with armed republicanism was long established. As far back as the 1950s, the mountains and lush forests that surrounded the village were a favourite venue for training camps. After the split from the Official IRA in 1970, the meeting which led to the formation of a command structure for the Provisionals is reputed to have taken place in a room above a pub in Ballinamore that was owned by the town's most famous resident, John Joe McGirl.

In more recent years Ballinamore had acquired something of a Dodge City reputation after arson attacks on a bus and a timber lorry during the Maze hunger strikes, when much anti-British feeling was aroused. On 13 May 1981 – the day after Francis Hughes became the second hungerstriker to die – Thomas McAloon, a truck driver from Fermanagh, crossed the border into Leitrim on his way to pick up a load from Mullingar, County Westmeath. As he drove through Ballinamore he was waved down by four armed and masked men and was ordered out of his cab. The lorry was doused in petrol and set alight. Nine days later – the night after Raymond McCreesh and Patsy O'Hara died – an English registered coach, which had brought eighteen Sheffield anglers to the town on a coarse fishing holiday, was burnt out in St Felim's Square, opposite the Garda station.

But if Ballinamore was synonymous with anything then it was the McGirl family name. John Joe was a local publican, undertaker, county councillor and old school republican, whose membership of the IRA stretched back to the bad old days of the 1930s, when the organisation was reduced to a fanatical rump who were largely irrelevant in the Irish Free State. In 1953 he joined Sinn Féin, and in 1957 was elected to the Dáil as an abstentionist candidate. He was active during the IRA Border Campaign and was jailed in 1961 after he was caught transporting ammunition in his hearse. He was a vice president of Sinn Féin and, despite being friendly with Gerry Adams, was on the same ideological wavelength as Ruairí Ó Brádaigh and the other southern traditionalists who were trying to stop the younger northern faction taking over the movement.

McGirl's nephew, Francie, was also a Volunteer, whose name was associated with one of the IRA's most spectacular operations. On 27 August 1979 the car he was driving was stopped at a routine Garda checkpoint in Granard, County Longford. In the passenger seat next to him was another IRA man, Thomas McMahon, a thirty-one year-old carpenter and father of two from Carrickmacross, County Monaghan. When questioned, they denied even knowing one another. McMahon claimed McGirl had stopped for him while he was thumbing a lift. McGirl seemed nervous. They were both arrested under Section 30 of the Offences Against the State Act on suspicion of being members of an illegal organisation.

Two hours later, while they were still in custody, a huge explosion blew apart a fishing boat belonging to the Queen's cousin, seventy-nine year-old Earl Louis Mountbatten, off the coast of Mullaghmore, County Sligo. Mountbatten, who was supreme commander of Allied Forces in South East Asia during the Second World War, died in the explosion, along with his grandson and two others. Forensic experts who examined the clothes of McGirl and McMahon found sand identical to that from Mullaghmore strand in their shoes and socks. Traces of nitroglycerine and ammonium nitrate – both components of gelignite – were found on their clothes. Flecks of green paint from the boat were also found on one of McMahon's boots and on his coat. McMahon, who was believed to be the bombmaker, was convicted of murder by the Special-Criminal Court. McGirl was acquitted because, despite the heavy circumstantial evidence, there was nothing to place him on the boat.

Ballinamore was a hive of republican activity, but what led the Gardaí to suddenly switch their entire focus there mystified the IRA. The claim that a number of well-known Provisionals had been spotted in the town was almost certainly a cover story to protect an informant. The previous weekend O'Callaghan had bumped into one of the Tralee men who'd made his way back to Kerry. He told him that the gang had Tidey hidden in a forest somewhere in Leitrim. From his description it sounded like the woods north of Ballinamore, where O'Callaghan had once operated a bomb-making factory. He phoned his Garda handler. On Monday, 12 December, Chief Superintendent Patrick Culligan, the man in charge of the investigation, chaired a special meeting at Garda headquarters, where it was decided to switch the entire focus of the hunt to Leitrim, especially the mountainous forest region close to the border.

❖❖❖

They came for John Joe McGirl on Friday morning 16 December. At 10am, members of the Special Task Force entered his pub through the front and back doors. He asked if they had a warrant and one was shown to him. They opened and read his mail. They leafed through a diary he kept for county council business. They found nothing, but they placed him under arrest anyway. He knew it was going to be a long forty-eight hours so he asked if he could collect some clothes before he was driven under heavy armed guard to Castleblayney, County Monaghan. Members of McGirl's family, as well as any locals the Gardaí considered likely to help the kidnappers escape, were picked up and placed in preventive custody just as the search of the forests north of Ballinamore got underway.

Chief Superintendent JJ McNally, who had spent virtually his entire Garda career chasing IRA Volunteers in the border region, was in overall command of the Ballinamore operation, which was given the seasonal codename of Operation Santa Claus. His team was divided into ten units, codenamed Rudolph One, Two, Three etc. Each unit was made up of a team leader, an inspector, two sergeants, a Garda with local knowledge, two uniformed Gardaí experienced in border searches, between five and seven detectives, nine or ten recruits from the Garda college in Templemore, County Tipperary and one member of the army to accompany each recruit. They were fanned out in a long line, with instructions to comb every inch of the dense forest north of Ballinamore, while the person on either end of the line maintained radio contact with the local Garda station, or 'Echo Base' as it was known for the operation.

Gardaí were already searching the handful of houses and buildings in Derrada, including a joinery where Francie McGirl's nineteen-year-old brother worked. Some time after 1pm, Joseph was spotted on the road. He was asked where he was going and replied that he was going to get his hair cut. He was arrested. At around the same time, Hugh Prior, a local farmer whose brother Bernie owned the joinery, was stopped by armed Gardaí and soldiers. He was taken out of his car, searched, arrested under Section 30 of the Offences Against the State Act and then ordered back into the front passenger seat of the car. A uniformed Garda got into the driver's seat and an armed member of the Special Branch sat in the back. They set off for the Garda station in Ballinamore.

It was almost two o'clock when the Rudolph Five team moved into Derrada Wood and began beating their way through the briars, brambles and thick undergrowth, none of them expecting to find anything, as it seemed too dense to be habitable. Then, unexpectedly, two Gardaí and a soldier came across a sheet of polythene stretched between two trees. It looked like it might be the roof of a hideout. They noticed movement, so they stopped in their tracks and radioed for backup.

Unaware of this development, Gary Sheehan, a Garda recruit not yet out of training college, and Private Patrick Kelly, an experienced soldier who had done several tours of duty in the Lebanon, were approaching the bunker from the opposite direction. Sheehan spotted a man dressed in green combat fatigues crouching next to a low earthen bank and cleaning what looked like an army-issue rifle. Sheehan presumed he was a member of the search team, but when he called out to him there was no answer. A Garda sergeant standing a few feet away sensed something was wrong and called for assistance.

What happened next remains a matter of conjecture more than twenty years later. All that can be stated as fact is that there was a burst of gunfire from somewhere, and in the confusion that followed, Sheehan was shot in the face and head, while Kelly took several bullets to his body. They both died instantly. Speculation persisted for years that one or both had been killed by friendly fire. In 2003, the Morris tribunal, which was set up to investigate Garda corruption in County Donegal, received a statement from a witness who claimed to have heard a Garda admitting responsibility for an accidental killing in the course of the Tidey rescue. It is easy to understand how it could have happened in the chaos of the moment. The wood was filled with young Garda rookies and soldiers, and with IRA men who were dressed and armed like soldiers. Most members of the Rudolph team were there simply as searchers and had no previous exposure to hostile fire. Most of the recruits weren't long out of their teens, and a large number were eventually escorted from the scene, sobbing, with blankets over their shoulders, suffering from trauma and shock. There was panic and confusion everywhere.

After the initial burst of fire, three men in balaclavas and army fatigues emerged from the bunker. They exchanged shots with members of Rudolph Five and a hand grenade was thrown, sending the searchers diving for cover and offering the gang a moment to escape. Tidey saw his opportunity too and charged headfirst through thick brambles to get away. The kidnappers split into pairs and ran in different directions. Two of them grabbed two unarmed Gardaí and a soldier and ordered them to run ahead of them, forming a human shield that let them reach the mouth of the woods. There they overpowered another Garda and two more soldiers who had been providing cover for the searchers. Once out of the woods, they took what weapons their hostages had and ran off. The other two kidnappers had already made their way to a local house, where they found a blue Opel Kadett with the keys in the ignition.

By now, at least two calls for reinforcements had been sent out, but it was a long time – two hours according to one account – before proper backup arrived. It was the IRA gang's good fortune that they had been discovered at lunchtime, when many of the Garda and army support vehicles were away collecting food for the search parties.

Tidey eventually emerged from the wood. An army private and two Garda recruits found him crawling through brambles on the edge of the forest, unrecognisable in his three-week-old, grey-flecked beard and the combat fatigues the gang had dressed him in. He gasped the words, 'Tidey ... hostage,' but from the way he was dressed he looked more like a member of the kidnap gang. There occurred what Gardaí euphemistically described as a 'physical exchange'. Tidey was forced to the ground, with his hands behind his head, searched and had his shoes removed before he was frogmarched through a field and towards the road.

The kidnappers regrouped, and by the time they sped past in the commandeered Kadett there were six of them in all, two in the front, two in the back and two taking up machine gun positions in the open boot. Tidey was being led through the field when they tore past and fired a number of times in his direction. Garda Donal Kelleher, who realised that Tidey was who he claimed to be, threw himself on top of him and was hit in the leg by a bullet. A Garda who was parked at a junction on the main road from

Derrada saw the gunmen approaching and swung his car into the middle of the road to block them off. They abandoned the car and took off across the fields towards the hills, each taking his turn every twenty yards or so to cover their backs by firing at pursuing Gardaí and soldiers.

A call was put out over the Garda radio to say that 'the Provos are shooting from a blue Opel car.' By an unfortunate quirk of fate, the car in which Hugh Prior was being driven by a Garda to Ballinamore for questioning was a light blue Ford Cortina. A Garda and army party on the other side of the woods mistook the Cortina for the stolen getaway car and opened fire on it. Prior was hit in the neck before the armed detective in the back shouted, 'Don't fire. There are armed Gardaí and a prisoner in this car.'

Tidey was taken in the back of a Garda car to Ballyconnell, County Cavan, where he made a phone call to his daughter, Susan, to tell her he was safe. Then, overcome by the emotion of the day, he was driven, with tears streaming down his face, back to his home in Dublin to be reunited with his family. The news that he was free was announced over the loudspeaker systems in Quinnsworth stores around the country and was met with spontaneous cheers and applause by shoppers. The British Prime Minister, Margaret Thatcher, sent a telegram of congratulations to Garret FitzGerald.

❖❖❖

The bodies of the dead soldier and the Garda recruit remained in Derrada Wood all night. An unexploded grenade lay close to the remains and there were also fears that the IRA had booby trapped the area around the bunker. Dusk was falling and it was decided to wait until first light to retrieve the bodies of Sheehan, a twenty-three year-old from Carrickmacross, County Monaghan, who was due to graduate from the Garda training school in a matter of weeks, and Kelly, a thirty-five year-old married man with four children from Moate, County Westmeath.

On Sunday, John Joe and Joseph McGirl, Hugh Prior and those arrested at the same time were all released without charge, as thousands of army and Garda personnel descended on Ballinamore to help in the search for the kidnappers. The army's Fourth Cavalry arrived from Longford. The Sixth Infantry came from Athlone. Several divisions of the Air Corps flew in from Casement Aerodrome, Baldonnel. Two Alouette and one Gazelle helicopter hovered permanently overhead, while armed detectives, soldiers and the commando-style Army Rangers, their faces blacked up, worked sixteen-hour days scouring the countryside for the kidnappers. The rangers were told that they could use 'maximum aggression' in pursuit of their quarry. 'Those guys don't want to be taken alive,' one told a journalist, 'and we're not interested in taking them alive.'

The security forces encountered a lot of local hostility. Some Gardaí claimed that they were called 'black bastards' by people in the area, while members of the Irish army said they were called 'Brits' and were refused service in some shops. Ted Nealon, a TD for the area, said that even those without republican sympathies felt compelled not to cooperate. 'Fear may prevent them from saying what they really mean,' he said.

The topography was even more hostile than the natives. There were thousands of square miles of dense forest and undergrowth, as well as caves, ravines and gullies that could provide cover for the fugitives. But the Gardaí were convinced that they had them pinned down inside a few square miles of forest and scrubland between Derrada and Benbrack mountain and would have them smoked out before Christmas.

The kidnappers outwitted them. The last that was seen of them was on Monday, 19 December, in the middle of the afternoon, when a detective spotted two men, and possibly a third, crawling through the woods at Ardmoneen. That night they slipped through the cordon and, by first light on Tuesday, four of the kidnappers were making their way through Sligo towards Mayo.

There they met up with Mary McGing, an engineer with Mayo County Council and a Sinn Féin activist. That week she spoke to Colman O'Reilly, a friend who worked as a teacher in Knock National School, and asked him if he had moved into the new house he'd bought in Claremorris. He said he hadn't and she asked if a few of her Sinn Féin friends who were in town for a meeting could stay there. O'Reilly took her story at face value and handed over the keys.

Some time in the evening of Tuesday, 20 December, Sergeant Desmond O'Rourke and two other Gardaí were operating a checkpoint at Ballyveeny Bridge near Ballycroy in west Mayo, looking for poitín smugglers. The road was as deserted as it usually was at that time of night. A white Mercedes approached and the sergeant flagged it down. McGing was driving. There were four men in the car with her. The one in the front seat had the hood of his anorak up and looked suspicious. O'Rourke shone his light into the back and noticed that one of the other men had the barrel of a gun between his knees. He flashed his lamp as a warning to the other Gardaí, then made a grab for the gun. As he did so, one of the other men, who was bearded, jumped out and pointed a machine gun at him. The others, all of whom had Northern accents, got out and tied the Gardaí up, using their belts. They forced them to lie face down on the road, then slashed the tyres of their car before escaping.

McGing took the men to the vacant house in Claremorris, where they ate and then slept. The following day, local Gardaí tracked down the gang to the house and surrounded it. The house was in darkness when they arrived. Sergeant Patrick Touhy from Castlebar went to the back door and heard a noise inside. He shouted at whoever was there to turn on the lights and throw out their guns. The front door was flung open and the men shot their way out of the house. This time they were gone for good.

Four days before Christmas, just after five o'clock in the evening, Gardaí arrived at the door of John Curnan, a fifty-eight year-old forester and farmer from just outside Balli-namore. He'd been expecting them. Curnan owned the woods where Tidey had been held captive. He admitted giving flasks of boiling water to someone he claimed was a complete stranger who approached him while he was cutting down Christmas tree on the day before the rescue. He was charged with falsely imprisoning Tidey and was jailed for seven years, the last five of which were suspended due to ill-health.

Two years later, Mick Burke walked into the Garda station in Tralee and gave himself up. A neighbour of Tidey's picked him out of a line-up as the man who had posed as a Garda at the fake checkpoint at Stocking Lane. He was sentenced to twelve years for false imprisonment. Billy Kelly, who hired the car used by the kidnappers, was jailed for three years.

On 5 January 1998, Brendan McFarlane, one of the IRA's leading figures, was arrested and charged with falsely imprisoning Tidey and possessing a firearm during the same period, with intent to endanger life. McFarlane, who was OC of the IRA prisoners during the 1981 hunger strike and a close friend of Bobby Sands, had led the Maze breakout in September 1983. Travelling under a false passport, he ended up in Europe and was eventually rearrested in Amsterdam in 1986, along with the London car bomber and 1975 hunger striker Gerry Kelly, and extradited to Northern Ireland. He had been freed on parole in 1997 and spent Christmas and New Year in Copenhagen with his Danish girlfriend. He flew back to Dublin and was on a coach travelling to Belfast to sign his full release papers when Gardaí stopped the bus just north of Dundalk and arrested him. It was alleged that McFarlane's fingerprints were found on a number of items, including a beer can, discovered in the bunker at Derrada Woods, but these items, it emerged, could no longer be found. The Gardaí had never requested his extradition from the North in relation to the kidnap nor arrested him during the many visits he made to the Republic while he was released on licence. In the High Court in July 2003, Mr Justice Ó Caoimh ruled that his right to a fair trial had been prejudiced by the delay in prosecuting and the loss of items on which Gardaí claimed his fingerprints were found. He ordered that the trial should not go ahead.

❖❖❖

In Ballinamore life returned to normal. In the days before Christmas the Gardaí and soldiers began to clear out and the locals got their village back after two weeks spent in the uncomfortable glare of the media spotlight. They returned to the issues that really affected their lives – money frittering across the border as people chased Christmas bargains, and the Government's failure to deliver a direct dial telephone service as promised. As late as 1983, making a local phone call in Ballinamore still required assistance from an operator.

A Sinn Féin Christmas cabaret in a local hotel, at which Gerry Adams, the newly elected Sinn Féin leader, was due to speak, was quietly cancelled, though not everyone treaded so sensitively. John Joe McGirl gave what became a famous interview to the *Leitrim Observer*, in which he said he was sorry that it was two Irishmen who'd been killed trying to save Tidey's life. 'I regret the death of the two Irishmen over an Englishman,' he said, 'but I'm certainly not going to get on the bandwagon of condemnations.' He stated that he had personal reservations about the policy of kidnapping for ransom that the IRA had adopted, but said that the organisation had always done its best to avoid armed clashes with the Republic's security forces.

On the weekend following the kidnapping, a Christmas message from the IRA flashed up on a giant neon sign in

Times Square in New York, offering season's greetings to all prisoners of war in Ireland and England. But it was a far from merry Christmas for the IRA, for whom the Maze escape was a rare highpoint in a dark year. The so-called supergrass system, under which Volunteers were 'turned' to help put away old friends and comrades, had sapped morale within the movement. In November there was a lot of painful bloodletting as Adams completed his takeover of Sinn Féin from the southern old guard, who were against money being diverted from the armed struggle into politics. Financially the IRA were close to broke and attempts to raise money through kidnapping had been a disaster, resulting in the deaths of two members of the Republic's security forces.

On 17 December, the day after Sheehan and Kelly were shot dead in Derrada Wood, an IRA unit detonated a car bomb outside Harrods department store in London in the middle of the Christmas shopping rush. Three policemen, an American tourist, a young mother and a journalist were killed. The IRA took the unusual step of saying that they regretted the deaths and that the operation was not author- ised by the Army Council. The bombing was blamed on hardline elements within the organisation who were attempting to derail the republican leadership's new prag- matic electoral strategy. But the political reaction to the Bal- linamore and Harrods killings was one of outrage. FitzGerald's government met to consider proscribing Sinn Féin. It was a mark of how low their standing had sunk that Fianna Fáil leader Charles Haughey – the man who once stood accused (but was acquitted) of arming the IRA – said he would offer no objection. 'If that's what the Government decide to do, with their full knowledge of the security situation,' he said, 'we will certainly support them.' The Northern Ireland secretary, Jim Prior, argued against proscription, saying that the party's exclusion from the political process would only help legitimise the IRA's military campaign.

Gerry Adams refused to condemn what had happened in Ballinamore. Though he regretted the deaths of Sheehan and Kelly, he said the IRA men involved in the operation were 'doing their duty.' But support for Sinn Féin in the Republic was shaken by the killings in Leitrim. According to one IRA man:

> There was a lot of soul-searching went on after that. The Harrods bombing was stupid. But the kidnappings were stupid as well. Practically every guard and soldier in the State was on our backs and all for a few quid. Between Shergar and then Tidey you couldn't move a finger that year. It made it impossible. Then you're taking people who aren't actually involved in the conflict and you're holding them hostage and you've got their wives and daughters and sons on the television, crying their hearts out. It costs you sympathy and support. And then it was inevitable that we were going to come into a conflict situation with the Gardaí or the army. It was completely stupid. It was like something from another age.

Many within the organisation associated kidnapping for ransom with the underworld and felt that it aided the British and Irish government's efforts to criminalise what they claimed was a legitimate political struggle. Mallon had his knuckles rapped for the three botched operations. He had the support of the IRA in Tyrone and might even have become a difficult adversary for Adams, but after 1983 he was never again of relevance within the republican movement.

❖❖❖

Just over a year later, there was an unexpected addendum to the Tidey story. Rumours persisted that the IRA continued to demand money from Associated British Foods long after Tidey's release. Early in 1985 it was discovered that £2m sterling had been paid into a Swiss bank account, from where £1.75m of it was transferred via New York to an account at the Bank of Ireland in Navan, County Meath. The money was earmarked for Sinn Féin's local election campaign that year. FitzGerald was tipped off about the money on 13 February and set to work drafting legislation to enable the State to seize it. He briefed Haughey, who promised to cooperate fully in ensuring that the law was enacted. The Bill was passed without opposition and received barely a mention in the newspapers. Then two men, Alan Clancy and David McCartney, instituted High Court proceedings, claiming that the money was theirs. They failed in their action. ABF denied that the money related to the Tidey kidnap. The transfer happened at a time when protection money was considered not just a fact of life but a tax deductible business expense for supermarkets operating in Northern Ireland. The Provisionals had discovered that extortion was a quieter and less messy way of making money than high profile kidnappings.

No honest audit of the ten-year period between the Thomas Niedermayer tragedy and the killings in Derrada Wood could conclude that kidnapping – whether for political reasons or for ransom – was anything other than a disaster for the republican movement. If money was indeed paid for Dunne's return, then it was a rare success. The Niedermayer case resulted in the death of a man who was no more than an innocent bystander in the Troubles. The abduction of Lord and Lady Donoughmore played no part at all in the decision to return the hunger-striking London bomb team to Northern Ireland. The long and protracted kidnapping of Tiede Herrema didn't persuade the Irish Government to release the three named IRA prisoners. The theft of Shergar cost the Provisionals credibility. The Weston abduction attempt cost them five Volunteers. And the Tidey kidnapping cost two lives.

And so, in the wild forests north of Ballinamore, where a soldier and a Garda lay dead among the brambles, the IRA decided they had taken their last hostage.

Bibliography

Bew, Paul and Gillespie, Gordon, *Northern Ireland, A Chronology of the Troubles 1968-1993*, Dublin, Gill & Macmillan, 1993.

Connolly, Colm, *Herrema: Siege at Monasterevin*, Dublin, Olympic Press, 1977.

Coogan, Tim Pat, *The IRA*, London, Harper Collins, 1995.

David, Roy, *The Shergar Mystery*, Manchester, Trainers Record, 1986.

Davidson, AJ, *Kidnapped*, Dublin, Gill & Macmillan, 2003.

Devlin, Paddy, *Straight Left: An Autobiography*, Belfast, The Blackstaff Press, 1993.

Harnden, Toby, Bandit *Country*, London, Hodder and Stoughton, 1999.

Kerrigan, Gene, *Round Up The Usual Suspects*, Dublin, Magill, 1985.

McKittrick, David; Kelters, Seamus; Feeney, Brian; and Thornton, Chris, *Lost Lives*, Edinburgh, Mainstream, 1999.

Moloney, Ed, *The Secret History of the IRA*, London, Allen Lane/The Penguin Press, 2002.

Murtagh, Peter and Joyce, Joe, *The Boss*, Dublin, Gill & Macmillan, 1983.

O'Brien, Brendan, *The Long War*, Dublin, The O'Brien Press, 1993.

O'Callaghan, Sean, *The Informer*, London, Corgi, 1998.

Rees, Merlyn, *Northern Ireland: A Personal Perspective*, London, Methuen, 1985.

Smyth, Sam, *Thanks a Million Big Fella*, Dublin, Blackwater Press, 1997.

Thompson, Derek, *Tommo's Year*, London, Boxtree, 1997.

Turner, Colin, *In Search of Shergar*, London, Sidgwick & Jackson, 1984.

Walsh, Liz, *The Final Beat: Gardaí Killed in the Line of Duty*, Dublin, Gill & Macmillan, 2001.

NEWSPAPERS AND PERIODICALS
The Irish Times
Irish Independent
Irish Press
Evening Press
Evening Herald
Sunday Independent
Sunday Press
Sunday Tribune
Cork Examiner
Leitrim Observer
Limerick Leader
Donegal Democrat
Racing Post
Magill Magazine
Belfast Telegraph
The Irish News
News Letter

MORE TRUE CRIME FROM THE O'BRIEN PRESS

THE JOY
Mountjoy Jail – The shocking, true story of life inside
Paul Howard

A no-holds-barred account of a criminal's time in the notorious Dublin prison, as revealed to journalist Paul Howard. This extraordinary story tells of the desperate lifestyle of a junkie; bullying and savage beatings among the prisoners; ingenious drug-smuggling ploys. But alongside the pain there is humour – from the hilarity of World Cup celebrations to the distraction of a beautiful aerobics teacher.

Paperback €9.95/STG£6.99

STAKEKNIFE
Britain's Secret Agents in Ireland
Greg Harkin and Martin Ingram

An explosive exposé of how British military intelligence really works – from the inside. The stories of two undercover agents: the man known as Stakeknife, Force Research Unit (FRU) agent and deputy head of the IRA's infamous 'Nutting Squad', the internal security force which tortured and killed suspected informers; and Brian Nelson, who also worked for the FRU, and aided loyalist terrorists and murderers in their bloody work.

Paperback €11.95/STG£8.99

DEATH IN DECEMBER
The Story of Sophie Toscan du Plantier
Michael Sheridan

On 23 December 1996, the body of Sophie Toscan du Plantier was discovered outside her remote holiday cottage near Schull in West Cork. The attack had been savage and merciless. The murder caused shockwaves in her native France and in the Cork countryside she had chosen as her retreat from her glamorous lifestyle in Paris. Despite an extensive investigation, the killer of Sophie is still at large … the file remains open. **Updated to include a day-by-day account of the sensational Ian Bailey libel case.**

Paperback €9.95/STG£6.99

THE GENERAL
Godfather of Crime
Paul Williams

Now a major motion picture by John Boorman.

In a twenty-year career marked by obsessive secrecy, brutality and meticulous planning, Martin Cahill, aka The General, netted over £40 million. He was untouchable – until a bullet from an IRA hitman ended it all. A compelling read, this book reveals Cahill's bizarre personality and the activities of the *Tango Squad* – the special police unit that targetted him using tactics employed against the infamous Kray Gang.

Paperback €9.95/STG£7.99

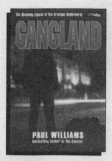

GANGLAND
Paul Williams

A compelling, chilling read, *Gangland* gives the inside story on a dark and sinister world. Who are the families that form the Irish mafia? What have been their most daring exploits? How do they hide their activities from the authorities? Williams examines the way in which they have spread their net across the country and beyond, reaping huge profits which allow them to live the high life while bringing misery to others.

Paperback €9.95/STG£6.99

Send for our full-colour catalogue